WE HAVE RECEIVED A
COMPLAINT

WE HAVE RECEIVED A
COMPLAINT

The Fraught World of Workplace Justice

MATT MALONE

SUTHERLAND
HOUSE

TORONTO, 2024

Sutherland House
416 Moore Ave., Suite 205
Toronto, ON M4G 1C9

First edition, February 2024

If you are interested in inviting one of our authors to a live event or
media appearance, please contact sranasinghe@sutherlandhousebooks.com
and visit our website at sutherlandhousebooks.com for more
information about our authors and their schedules.

We acknowledge the support of the Government of Canada.

Manufactured in Turkey
Cover designed by Lena Yang and Jordan Lunn
Book composed by Karl Hunt

Library and Archives Canada Cataloguing in Publication
Title: We have received a complaint : the fraught world of workplace justice / Matt Malone.
Names: Malone, Matt (Assistant professor of law), author.
Identifiers: Canadiana (print) 20230596304 | Canadiana (ebook) 20230596320 |
ISBN 9781990823626 (softcover) | ISBN 9781990823619 (EPUB)
Subjects: LCSH: Labor discipline. | LCSH: Organizational justice.
Classification: LCC HD6971.3 .M35 2024 |
DDC 658.3/14—dc23/eng/20231120 | 658.3/14—dc23

ISBN 978-1-990823-62-6
eBook 978-1-990823-61-9

CONTENTS

INTRODUCTION

It started, of course, on X (formerly Twitter).

"Name the worst job you ever had," prompted a tweet in the early afternoon of December 5, 2020.

Three minutes later, Manhattan Borough presidential candidate Lindsey Boylan, a former deputy secretary and special advisor to New York governor Andrew Cuomo, fired off her response.[1]

"Most toxic team environment?" she wrote. "Working for @NYGovCuomo."[2] In a long thread, she described: "If people weren't deathly afraid of him, they'd be saying the same thing and you'd already know the stories. Seriously, the messages and texts I receive when I speak the truth about this . . . it's a whole book of people who have been harmed."[3]

Observers took notice. The following day, the *Daily Mail* ran a story on Boylan's tweet.[4] Prior to that, Boylan had cut a mostly minor media figure. Her unsuccessful bid earlier that year to oust the US representative Jerry Nadler in the Democratic primary for New York's 10th congressional district had gained relatively little attention.[5] Two weeks prior to tweeting about Cuomo, she had announced her candidacy for Manhattan Borough President, but that, too, had failed to drum up much notice or support.[6] She ultimately placed fourth.[7]

Things now seemed about to change. In the days after her tweet and the *Daily Mail* article, Boylan's X account gained one thousand new followers. To these new arrivals, she plugged her ongoing campaign.[8] However, over the following week, media attention faded. There were no more news stories.

Cuomo showed little concern about the potential fallout from allegations of fostering a toxic workplace environment. He had little reason to be worried. Earlier that year, he had registered approval ratings of 77 percent.[9] Only a couple weeks before Boylan's tweet, the International Academy of Television Arts and Sciences had broken with tradition and awarded him the first Emmy to a sitting politician for his daily COVID-19 media briefings.[10] He was considered a leading nominee for *Time*'s Person of the Year.[11] News stories were still circulating that President Biden was considering naming Cuomo as his attorney general.[12]

On December 13, 2020, Boylan took to X again, this time spontaneously tweeting from the passenger seat of her car while her husband was driving.[13] "@NYGovCuomo sexually harassed me for years," she wrote. "Many saw it, and watched."[14]

She added: "I've been getting all these messages from people I won't be sharing, because it's their truth, but I must say, @NYGovCuomo will go down as one of the biggest abusers of all time."[15]

These allegations gained far more attention. Boylan garnered over 15,000 new followers on X.[16] The following day, *The New York Times* profiled the tweet,[17] highlighting the contrast between the nature of the allegations and recent reforms to the state's sexual harassment laws, which Cuomo had introduced in the wake of the #MeToo movement.[18] These laws required employers to adopt and distribute sexual harassment policies and train employees on sexual harassment.[19]

In public, Cuomo issued a terse denial about the allegations and appeared sanguine. In private, his team sought to discredit Boylan. They drafted and circulated for signature an op-ed letter casting Boylan in a negative light.[20] It emphasized her purported links to Donald Trump and stated: "Weaponizing a claim of sexual harassment for personal political gain or to achieve notoriety cannot be tolerated. False claims demean the veracity of credible claims."[21] The chair of Time's Up, an organization founded by Hollywood women to fight sexual abuse and promote gender equality, reviewed the letter.[22] The executive director of the Human Rights Campaign, the nation's largest LGBTQ advocacy organization, also reviewed it and circulated it for signatures.[23] The letter was never released.

Over the next two months, Boylan's allegations once again faded from public view.[24] Then, on February 24, 2021, she took to *Medium*, an online publishing platform, to release a 1,757-word entry entitled "My story of working with Governor Cuomo." It began:

> "Let's play strip poker."
> I should have been shocked by the Governor's crude comment, but I wasn't.
> We were flying home from an October 2017 event in Western New York on his taxpayer-funded jet. He was seated facing me, so close

our knees almost touched. His press aide was to my right and a state trooper behind us.

"That's exactly what I was thinking," I responded sarcastically and awkwardly. I tried to play it cool. But in that moment, I realized just how acquiescent I had become.

Governor Andrew Cuomo has created a culture within his administration where sexual harassment and bullying is so pervasive that it is not only condoned but expected. His inappropriate behavior toward women was an affirmation that he liked you, that you must be doing something right. He used intimidation to silence his critics. And if you dared to speak up, you would face consequences.[25]

In the subsequent investigation, Howard Zemsky, the CEO of Empire State Development, the umbrella organization for New York's two principal economic development public-benefit corporations, later corroborated that he heard Cuomo make the "strip poker" comment. He also corroborated that Boylan had sent him a text around the time of her December tweets stating: "I can't wait to destroy your life, you shit follower."[26]

In the *Medium* piece, Boylan went on to allege Cuomo had nonconsensually kissed her on the lips. During the subsequent investigation, Cuomo denied this specific allegation but admitted that he "may,"[27] on occasion, have kissed staff members on the lips.[28] The investigation found a kiss took place.[29] In her article, Boylan also revealed two women had reached out to her in December to share their own experiences and fears of speaking out.[30] She concluded: "I hope that sharing my story will clear the path for other women to do the same."[31]

This is precisely what happened.

As the story became a regular item in the news,[32] a second[33]—and then a third[34]—woman came forward in the media with new allegations. One of these women alleged Cuomo had asked her unwanted questions about her sex life, including whether she had "ever been with an older man."[35] The other woman alleged he touched her back, then "placed his hands on her cheeks" and asked if he could kiss her.[36]

By this point, the story had turned into a full-blown scandal, receiving regular front-page attention. In response, Cuomo issued an apology for any interactions or comments that "have been misinterpreted as unwanted flirtation" and underscored that he had "learned an important lesson."[37] In the days after this apology, New York State Senator Liz Krueger and

New York City mayoral candidates Dianne Morales, Maya Wiley, and Andrew Yang made calls for an independent investigation.[38] Another state representative called on him to resign.[39]

Cuomo bowed to the calls for an investigation. He suggested a retired federal judge lead it. After this proposal was rebuffed, he floated letting New York Attorney General Letitia James and Chief Judge of the New York Court of Appeals Janet DiFiore—both Cuomo appointees—jointly decide on an independent investigator. James rejected this suggestion, stating she wanted sole authority to appoint the investigator.[40] Cuomo agreed to this request.[41] James promised to hire an outside law firm and deputize private lawyer-investigators as state attorneys with the power to issue subpoenas.[42]

A week later, she announced as lead investigators Joon H. Kim from the law firm Cleary Gottlieb Steen & Hamilton LLP and Anne L. Clark from the law firm Vladeck, Raskin & Clark, P.C. They were hired at a discounted rate of $750 per hour,[43] with members of their respective law firm teams billing between $325 and $575 per hour.[44] James' office would go on to spend approximately $3.2 million in legal fees on the investigation.[45]

As the investigation got underway, public pressure continued to mount. By March 12, 2021, US Senate Majority Leader Charles Schumer and New York Senator Kirsten Gillibrand were calling on Cuomo to step down.[46] When President Biden was asked about his opinion of Cuomo staying in office, he stated: "I think the investigation is underway, and we should see what it brings us."[47] Cuomo himself oscillated between pleading for due process and taking an aggressive posture—at one point even retorting, "people know the difference between playing politics, bowing to cancel culture, and the truth."[48] A headline story in *The New York Times* the following day described: "The Imperious Rise and Accelerating Fall of Andrew Cuomo."[49] The paper's editorial board asked: "Can Andrew Cuomo continue to lead?"[50]

By mid-March, six women had come forward in the media to raise allegations about sexual harassment or other inappropriate behavior.[51] Attention also shifted from the substance of the allegations to Cuomo's behavior in response to the complainants coming forward. On March 16, *The New York Times* broke the story about the op-ed discrediting Boylan that Cuomo had helped draft with his staff, the chair of Time's Up, and the executive director of the Human Rights Campaign. Later that week, Ronan Farrow, who had recently shared the 2018 Pulitzer Prize for his reporting on film mogul Harvey Weinstein's predations on women, published a piece in *The New Yorker* detailing the campaign to discredit Boylan. Cuomo's spokesperson, he wrote, had leaked Boylan's personnel file to tarnish her reputation.[52]

By May, several complainants had received subpoenas for interviews.[53] In July, Cuomo himself was interviewed in his office on the 39th floor of 633 3rd Ave;[54] the interview lasted eleven hours.[55] In Cuomo's testimony to the investigators, he alleged a connection between one or more of the complainants and Attorney General Letitia James' office. This information was redacted from the transcript of Cuomo's interview when James' office subsequently published it.[56] One of Cuomo's lawyers later alleged James' chief of staff, Ibrahim Khan, had "been coordinating" with Boylan.[57]

In total, the investigators issued seventy subpoenas for documents that amassed over 74,000 records. The investigative team interviewed 179 individuals, including forty-one under oath. Among them was Cuomo's brother, CNN anchor Chris Cuomo.[58]

Finally, on August 3, 2021, James released the report.[59] It found Cuomo had engaged in "unwelcome and nonconsensual touching" and made "numerous offensive comments of a suggestive and sexual nature" against staff, public servants, and members of the public.[60] The investigators concluded, among other findings, Cuomo had grabbed an employee's breast,[61] asked about a potential reassignment into his protective unit for a female trooper who lacked requisite job qualifications (she was then assigned to his unit),[62] and told another employee that he was "lonely" and "wanted to be touched."[63] The investigators also noted his office's response to the complaints was "improper and inadequate."[64]

"This is a sad day for New York," said James, as she announced the release of the report, "because independent investigators have concluded Governor Cuomo sexually harassed multiple women and, in doing so, broke the law."[65] The report concluded Cuomo had engaged in the harassment of eleven women in total and created a hostile work environment for others.[66] President Biden finally joined the calls for Cuomo to step down.[67]

Cuomo gave his resignation speech a week later. "In my mind," he said at the time, "I have never crossed the line with anyone. But I didn't realize the extent to which the line has been redrawn."[68] The International Academy of Television Arts and Sciences rescinded his Emmy the following week.[69] On August 24, 2021, Lieutenant Governor of New York Kathy Hochul replaced Cuomo as the fifty-seventh governor of the state on an interim basis, pending an election. The day following Cuomo's resignation, James said the investigation closed "a sad chapter for all of New York, but it's an important step towards justice." She thanked Cuomo for his service.[70]

The following day, *The New York Times* ran a story on possible successors to Cuomo and noted that "the most significant question" was whether James, fresh off administering the investigation, would run for governor.[71] Shortly thereafter, U-Haul trucks arrived at the Governor's Executive Mansion on Eagle Street in Albany to clear out Cuomo's personal effects.[72] In early September, James was seen at the New York State Fairgrounds, in a move widely acknowledged as an opportunity for governor hopefuls to gain attention.[73] The following month, she began a statewide tour to distribute money to fight the opioid epidemic in a media blitz again noted for its publicity.[74]

On October 27, 2021, *The New York Times* reported James' aides, including her chief of staff, Ibrahim Khan, were quietly informing allies that James would run for governor.[75] That same day, the Albany County Sheriff filed a misdemeanor complaint against Cuomo for touching one of the complainants, as described in the investigative report (the charge was dismissed in January 2022).[76] The following day, James announced she was running for governor. "I've held accountable those who mistreat and harass women in the workplace," she stated in her announcement speech, alluding to her work administering the Cuomo investigation, "no matter how powerful the offenders."[77]

In November, James' office released transcripts of the investigators' interview with Cuomo's brother Chris. Reports revealed Chris Cuomo had joined the governor's strategy calls in response to Boylan's public complaints and had leveraged media contacts to go after complainants, including chasing a secondhand tip suggesting one of the complainants was lying.[78] On November 30, CNN suspended Chris Cuomo pending an investigation. The next day, a sexual harassment complaint against Chris Cuomo emerged. Three days later, CNN fired him.[79]

After polls showed James trailing Hochul, James stepped out of the race for governor.[80] Prosecutors in Nassau, Westchester, Albany, and Oswego counties then declined to bring forward any new prosecutions against Cuomo for claims related to conduct described in the investigative report.[81]

In early 2022, two of the complainants then filed civil suits by themselves.[82] Their claims still languish in the formal justice system and have gained almost no media attention.[83] Cuomo's fees in one of the lawsuits were completely covered by the state, as a judge found the allegations occurred while Cuomo "was acting within the scope of his employment or duties."[84] In that suit, Cuomo has subpoenaed at least five of the women from the investigation, including Boylan, for "records of communications the women had with investigators and reporters before going public with their claims."[85] In the other lawsuit, Cuomo was permitted to use the remaining campaign funds to pay his legal fees. He had $18 million when he left office.[86]

In spring 2022, Cuomo spent hundreds of thousands of dollars on a TV advertising campaign to present himself as a victim[87] and repeated claims that he was a target of "cancel culture."[88] In September 2022, he filed a forty-eight-page ethics complaint with the state bar against James and the investigators, which claimed James had "cynically manipulated a legal process for personal, political gain."[89] Among other things, Cuomo claimed James' refusal to disavow running for governor placed her in a conflict of interest in organizing the investigation.[90] Two months after he filed this complaint, James was reelected to her position with 55 percent of the vote in the November 2022 election.[91]

The following month, James' chief of staff, Ibrahim Khan, suddenly resigned after being faced with sexual harassment allegations relating to his "inappropriate touching and unwanted kissing" of two women.[92] The first complainant to come forward had worked on James' 2018 election campaign for attorney general, when the conduct was alleged to have occurred.[93] Khan was also the subject of another complaint in 2017 by a former employee of James' office, who "had accused him of drugging and sexually assaulting her at a holiday party."[94] Following media attention, James enlisted a law firm to conduct an independent investigation.[95]

This was not good enough for some of James' critiques. "There must be an immediate, independent investigation," said Republican State Senator Tom O'Mara, dismissing the investigation James had commissioned, "about what she knew about these allegations, when she knew it, and if they were properly addressed."[96] O'Mara's point was clear. Who investigates, how they investigate, and what they investigate can always change. There is little to lose in calling for the process to start all over again from the beginning.

Cuomo is now rumored to be contemplating a run for the Senate in 2024.[97]

What, one might ask, was the point of any of this?

And who came out of this spectacle in good form? What kind of justice was delivered to the complainants, the respondent, and anyone else involved? The initial complaint was tainted by Boylan's potential interest in gaining attention for her own political campaign. The individual administering the investigation, James, later overtly coveted a political office that the investigation she administered impacted her chances of obtaining. She also displayed a very different approach to her response to allegations against her own chief of staff accused of drugging and sexually assaulting a woman. Cuomo himself deserved no better. He admitted he "may" have kissed some of his employees on the lips, and most of the allegations were widely corroborated, while his decision to go after Boylan's credibility through scurrilous means spoke to the arrogance of power. As for the investigation, its scope shape-shifted in disturbing ways, expanding to include allegations of retaliation while strenuously redacting relevant communications that spoke to the bias or conduct of other parties. The process cost millions.

Now the whole thing is being litigated anyway.

The result was a workplace investigation that had little to do with justice. It is telling that the only formal claims in the justice system brought forward by complainants relating to Cuomo's conduct still languish there and have received none of the time, attention, or haste of the workplace investigation itself. But the costs continue to run up. Few listened to the complainants or their complaints. Few bothered to engage in the hypothetical exercise of changing the roles of the parties at different intervals along the way to assess whether the process was characterized by fairness and due process.

None of this bodes well.

Calls for investigations like the one into Cuomo's conduct have become a favored cure-all in the workplace. Where parties want to defer responsibility, an investigation can stall blame. Where parties disagree over the truth, an investigation can promise to deliver it objectively. The impulse to demand an investigation has become instinctive, unrelenting, and pervasive. It can even seem venerable in an era where the fiercest battles in the public realm are over the truth. In disagreements today, where it is standard practice to dismiss not just opposing viewpoints but irritant facts as fake news, conspiracy theories, and misinformation, the truth is a valuable commodity. But do workplace investigations actually deliver truth, responsibility, or justice?

That is the question I address in this book.

CHAPTER ONE

INFORMAL JUSTICE

Workplace investigations are having a moment. They compel headlines in industries as diverse as entertainment,[1] sports,[2] politics,[3] technology,[4] healthcare,[5] and nearly every other field. With their promises to obtain responsibility, truth, and justice, workplace investigations have an undeniable pull at a time when these qualities are so often lacking in our public discourse. They seek to end fraught disputes by imposing order and fairness to ascertain the facts. It is no surprise, then, that in so many disputes, calling for an investigation is often the first or only thing parties can agree upon.

Against this backdrop, the device of the workplace investigation—the independent, objective, neutral process of fact-finding and, in some cases, the process of making policy or legal determinations based on those findings—has gained unique importance. But even as demands for such investigations have increased, they remain poorly understood. Few grasp why employers conduct them sometimes but not other times. Even fewer understand how they are conducted. They are seldom regulated by governments. While many jurisdictions have rules that give rise to workplace investigations, few have rules about how such investigations should occur.

This is a little book about the phenomenon, a discussion of the meat and guts of workplace investigations, written by someone who has conducted hundreds of them. I work as a law professor now, mainly researching how the law protects secret information in various contexts, but I am also interested in legal issues pertaining to modern workplaces, especially workplace investigations. From time to time, I still conduct investigations, although now I mostly review other investigators' work. Previously, I was a full-time workplace investigator at a law firm in California, where I conducted investigations all over the state and country in just about every type of workplace, including governments, Fortune 100 companies, universities, start-ups, sports teams, schools, charities, corporate C-suites, landmark and historical sites, and elsewhere. I have conducted workplace investigations into just about every type of complaint.

Even though the job of a workplace investigator is quite narrow—gathering evidence pertaining to specific allegations and evaluating and weighing that evidence using the preponderance of evidence to make factual determinations—I have often felt that the work raises broader questions about the nature of justice today, especially when compared with another place we often go to seek justice: court.

Consider some of the contrasts between the formal justice of courts and the informal justice of workplace investigations:

- In the formal justice system, parties have to reckon with concrete guardrails when they bring forward a claim, such as a limitation period. In a workplace investigation, allegations need not be time bound to activate an employer's concern.
- In the formal justice system, complaints must be drafted according to basic standards of pleading.[6] The onus is on the complaining party to draft allegations clearly and in a way that enables judges to grant relief.[7] Complaints should be "simple, concise, and direct."[8] By contrast, in workplace investigations, complaints might be vague, unclear, and confused. They may contain only a hint of a problem. And they might come from anywhere, like X.
- In the formal justice system, there are strict rules of evidence to abide by. In workplace investigations, such rules are eminently flexible.
- In the formal justice system, one-sided communications with the judge made without notice to all parties and not on the public record are permitted only in the most exceptional circumstances. In workplace investigations, such communications happen all the time. They are encouraged.
- In the formal justice system, there are tools to sanction vexing behavior. In workplace investigations, taking such measures risks being seen as retaliatory.
- In the formal justice system, anonymous complaints are not tolerated. In workplace investigations, anonymity is often permitted as a courtesy to complainants to enhance their willingness to come forward. Investigations might begin with Blind, an anonymous forum and

community reporting app, or through screenshots of texts delivered anonymously to a human resources department through the mail.[9]

As the foregoing makes clear, there are many differences between the way the formal justice system of courts and the informal justice system of workplace investigations operate. But formality is not always synonymous with producing justice. Courts can fail where workplace investigations can succeed.

The question I am interested in addressing is how, and how often, workplace investigations succeed. Despite the many problems with the formal justice system, it remains one of the most respected institutions in many liberal democracies. In the United States, public confidence in state courts (approximately 60 percent) outstrips public confidence in public schools (28 percent), large technology companies (26 percent), or newspapers (16 percent)—to say nothing of major corporations (11 percent), whom we now often ask to carry out workplace investigations.[10]

By contrast, and as the Cuomo investigation shows, even though most people may agree at the outset that a workplace investigation is desirable, its legitimacy once underway and after it concludes is often a question of fierce debate.

What is a workplace investigation? At its core, it is a complaint. Some are written; others are verbal. Some are short and clear; others emerge in whispers or inadvertently. Once the employer hears the complaint, they assess the attendant risks. Does the substance of the complaint expose them to liability? If they ignore the complaint, are they flouting an important legal obligation to create and maintain workplaces that meet a certain standard? If they terminate an employee due to the nature of the allegations, do they risk a lawsuit from the employee for doing so without proper grounds? And, perhaps most importantly, do they have enough information?

If the employer determines that an investigation is obligated by law or necessary for these reasons, they may engage a workplace investigator. This person might be an internal employee or a third party, such as a lawyer. The workplace investigator is charged with searching for the truth and making findings about disputed facts. Given how expansive the search for truth can be, the process requires parameters around what is (and isn't) being investigated and how it will be kept manageable and proportionate. I will examine some of these aspects in more detail later.

Then the investigation begins. Although every investigation is different, the investigator generally starts by reviewing the complaint, mapping the workplace, and examining any relevant and available documents. Then they prepare questions and conduct interviews, usually first with the complainant and then with witnesses. The respondent is usually interviewed last, once all the evidence has been gathered, so the respondent has an opportunity to respond to all accusations or claims against them. Once these stages are complete, some type of report is prepared. The report usually contains information about uncontested facts (job titles, dates, and places), and then it makes findings about contested items.

A report should explain why it draws the conclusions it does, showing its work and assessing the credibility of parties. Was a piece of evidence corroborated by multiple documents or witnesses? Did a party make consistent or inconsistent statements? Did a party have or lack an opportunity to observe the facts they are describing? What about their past history, bias, motive to lie, or reputation for veracity or deceit? And what about the sheer plausibility of their assertions? As a standard practice, the demeanor of parties is generally not given much consideration.

Once the report is done, that is the last word. The workplace investigator makes findings of fact, while the employer decides what to do with those findings. Once the investigator clicks "Send" on a report, the job is done. The search for facts is neutral. What happens with them afterwards is rarely so.[11]

CHAPTER TWO

RESPONSIBILITY

In July 2021, CBC News published a bombshell story about Julie Payette, the Governor General of Canada, the federal vice-regal representative of the Canadian monarch, and the highest-ranking individual in the country. An engineer, pilot, computer scientist, and astronaut who had served on two Space Shuttle missions and received honorary degrees from twenty-four Canadian universities, Payette was the definition of an eminent Canadian. The report was explosive.

The news article revealed allegations that Payette had created "a toxic climate of harassment and verbal abuse at Rideau Hall," her official residence and principal workplace. "This has gone from being one of the most collegial and enjoyable work environments for many of the staff to being a house of horrors," the article quoted one anonymous source as saying. "It's bullying and harassment at its worst." The allegations in the article stated Payette had engaged in yelling, belittling, and publicly humiliating employees, including throwing aside an employee's work on one occasion and calling it "shit."[1]

Prime Minister Justin Trudeau, who advised Queen Elizabeth II to appoint Payette, offered no support for her in response to the allegations.[2] His office put out a press release underscoring that every Canadian employee has a right to a "healthy, respectful and safe environment."[3] A month later, his government hired Quintet Consulting Corporation, a firm with "expertise in the field of conflict management and prevention, including conducting administrative investigations,"[4] to look into the complaints.[5]

As part of its investigation, Quintet interviewed seventy individuals with work histories at Rideau Hall, including forty-one current employees and twenty-nine former employees (all virtually, due to the pandemic).[6] The investigation was brisk and wrapped up within four months. On

January 12, 2021, Quintet submitted its Final Review Report,[7] in which forty-three interviewees described their work environment as "hostile" and twenty-six as "toxic" or "poisoned."[8] Even though the report did not make factual findings—it merely collected survey data directly from the interviewees themselves and highlighted various government policies that might be relevant in light of their statements—it encouraged the government to act "quickly and decisively"[9] to assure the "health and safety" of employees in the workplace.[10]

The report immediately captured national attention[11] and quickly led to Payette stepping down.[12] Her resignation statement began:

> Everyone has a right to a healthy and safe work environment, at all times and under all circumstances. It appears this was not always the case at the Office of the Secretary to the Governor General. Tensions have arisen at Rideau Hall over the past few months and for that, I am sorry.[13]

While there is much to be said about the sincerity and meaning of acts of apology in our present day, the more intriguing item in the government's, Quintet's, and Payette's declarations was the constant refrain of protecting employees' health and safety in the workplace. Although this appears to be an unqualified good, an obvious question arises.

What, exactly, is a healthy and safe workplace?

One way to answer this question is by looking at the past.

Workplaces were once shockingly dangerous environments. In the 1880s, some 15,000 Chinese came to Canada to build the Canadian Pacific Railway through its most dangerous pass across the Rocky Mountains from Calgary to Vancouver. Four percent of them died doing so. As CBC summarizes, "[o]ne worker died for every mile of track [laid] through the Rocky Mountains between Calgary and Vancouver."[14] The construction of the Panama Canal at the turn of the twentieth century killed tens of thousands of workers during its construction. Many architectural marvels also came at a harrowing human cost, and not long ago. Eight workers died building the Titanic. The Empire State Building, finished in 1930 within just a year, took the lives of fourteen construction workers. The official death toll of construction workers on the Hoover Dam, built between 1931 and 1936, was ninety-six. Even in the early 1970s, sixty workers died during the construction of the World Trade Center.

While workplace fatalities remain all too common, they are far less common than they once were. Even the most cynical reading of the available data shows there has been a tremendous advance in workplace health and safety over the last hundred years. The Center for Disease Control's *Morbidity and Mortality Weekly Report* has noted that in 1906–1907, 195 steelworkers died in work-related accidents in just one county in the United States (Allegheny County in Pennsylvania); by 1995, the number was seventeen steelworkers nationwide.[15] In 1900, 2,550 railway workers died on the job;[16] in 2021, the number was thirty-three.[17] In 1920, 2,272 workers died in coal mine accidents; in 2020, it was five.[18]

Broader trends tell the same story of workplaces in the United States becoming, on balance, far safer and healthier places. This is not to say that tragedies in the workplace do not still happen. Of course, they still do, but at a far lower rate than they once occurred. Across the United States, in 1970, an average of thirty-eight people per day died on the job.[19] Forty years later, in 2010, the average was thirteen. The National Safety Council, which was founded in 1913, in part, to record information about workplace fatalities, has shown that, in 1921, workplace fatalities claimed between 18,000 and 21,000 lives in the United States.[20] A hundred years later, it was 4,472.[21] These declines occurred even as the general population grew by over 200 million during the same period. Professor Steven Pinker has noted that, in 1913, the workplace fatality rate was sixty-one per 10,000 employees; in 2015, it was 3.2.[22] North American workplaces are safer and healthier than ever before.

What has been behind this steep drop in the rate of workplace fatalities? For many labor organizations and unions, the answer is clear. It traces back to 1970, when the Nixon administration passed the Occupational Safety and Health Act (OSHA). In addition to creating a regulatory agency and a national workplace health and safety research institute, OSHA replaced a jumble of systems for reporting workplace fatalities and injuries, enhancing transparent reporting.[23] Its goal was to assure "every working man and woman in the nation safe and healthful working conditions and to preserve our human resources."[24]

What came to be known as the "general duty" clause established that every employer "shall furnish to each of his employees' employment and a place of employment which are *free from recognized hazards that are causing or are likely to cause death or serious physical harm to his employees* [emphasis added]."[25] This duty carried an implicit obligation to investigate health and safety issues. As the eponymous agency administering OSHA made clear: "OSHA strongly encourages employers to investigate all incidents in which a worker was hurt, as well as close calls (sometimes called 'near misses'), in which a worker might have been hurt if the circumstances had been slightly different."[26]

This legislation went on to be mirrored in many other jurisdictions.[27] Shortly after it came into force, Canada's first occupational health and safety legislation was introduced in 1972.[28] The United Kingdom introduced its Health and Safety at Work Act in 1974.[29] This flurry of legislative change across the democratic world—embodied and driven by developments in American law, which I draw on for most examples in this chapter—was supported by judiciaries that actively affirmed employees' rights to refuse unsafe work. In the United States, in the landmark case *Whirlpool Corp* v. *Marshall* (1980), the Supreme Court held that employees at the Whirlpool Corporation facility in Marion, Ohio, were permitted to refuse work at a job station where, only a few weeks earlier, a coworker had fallen to his death through wiring that was still not reinforced by the employer.[30]

The resulting change since the 1970s has been remarkable. In the 1980s alone, occupational mortality decreased by 37 percent.[31] Today, in the United States, workplace suicides are more common than workplace deaths through fire or explosion, electrocution, or inhalation of a harmful substance.[32] Historically common causes of workplace fatalities such as being struck by a falling object or compressed by or caught by equipment have been replaced by the decidedly more modern phenomenon of being shot by a colleague.[33] (The most common site for mass shootings is the shooter's workplace or former workplace, according to the Violence Project.)[34] That said, the likelihood of such acts occurring is statistically nowhere near historic rates of fatalities in the workplace.

While many labor organizations and unions credit OSHA for improvements in worker health and safety, there is an important caveat to this story: OSHA did not come with much enforcement by the government. Its real impact came from the dissemination of rules enforced by employers themselves. OSHA was never zealous about enforcement.[35] For example, the AFL-CIO, the largest federation of unions in the United States, has noted that the federal government has only prosecuted 99 cases under the legislation, "with defendants serving a total of 112 months in jail."[36] These statistics are low for legislation that applies to almost every employer in the country.[37]

Instead of enforcement, OSHA downloaded regulations on employers through the duty to investigate. Employers became its main enforcers. OSHA accomplished this by using the threat of penalties. The penalty for a "serious" violation of OSHA requirements, including one that results in death, is currently $15,625. However, the penalty for a "willful" violation of the code is currently $156,259.[38] With thousands of potential violations in the code, the risk of liability can be significant when an employer becomes aware of a violation, that is, the moment their violation becomes "willful." It is fear of these penalties, more than actual enforcement, that has motivated the massive change in workplace health and safety.

Yet OSHA has not been without its problems, including a tendency toward overregulation that makes true compliance elusive, if not impossible. Philip K. Howard, a fierce critic of the framework, has noted: "OSHA itself has estimated that 80 percent of workplaces are not in compliance with the law. It has to be true that no one is in full compliance: Even on paper an accountant couldn't comply with four thousand rules. Is your supply closet neatly organized so that everything is 'stable and secure,' as required by Section 1910.176(b)? Have you checked recently?"[39]

Much of the difficulty of complying with OSHA today has to do with the dizzying growth in the number of regulations that make compliance only possible for the most sophisticated employers, a state of affairs that might be contributing to the concentration of corporate power that now characterizes the modern economy. When Howard was invited to OSHA to suggest reforms, he immediately proposed reducing the number of regulations. This was rejected. Howard then asked the large roomful of attendees whether any of them had read in its entirety the code they were responsible for enforcing. None had.[40]

Workplace health and safety laws are only part of the story. The delegation of responsibility for preventing harm and danger from physical threats has been followed by another important change: downloading obligations on employers to ward off discrimination and harassment in the workplace. In the United States, Title VII of the Civil Rights Act of 1964 outlawed discrimination based on race, color, religion, sex, and national origin in one's employment,[41] as well as harassment on these bases.[42] In addition to Title VII's application to nearly every employer,[43] Title IX also prohibited sex-based discrimination in education programs receiving federal government funding. It applies to nearly every educational institution in the country.

Like OSHA, these statutes were widely copied by other jurisdictions with fair employment practices legislation. They also came with enforcement bodies. Title VII is enforced by the Equal Employment Opportunity Commission (EEOC), while the Office of Civil Rights (OCR) enforces Title IX. As enforcement bodies, neither has performed well. Instead, their enforcement practices have largely been characterized by politics, depending on the administration in power at any given time. Between 1982 and 1990, during the Reagan administration, the EEOC shifted its focus from collective action to narrow enforcement under Chair Clarence Thomas.[44] During the Clinton administration, it acted with heavy-handed super-intention, pouring resources into cases like its unsuccessful action against Hooters for discriminating against men.[45]

Like the EEOC, the OCR channels the priorities and attitudes of the presidential administration in power at any given time. Under the Obama administration, the OCR presided over a major change in the regulation of sexual activity between students by telling educational institutions to use the preponderance of evidence, the lowest possible standard of proof, in sexual assault cases between students.[46] The consequences of this shift were far-reaching: "he-said, she-said" disputes where the only evidence was the credibility of two parties to a sexual act suddenly became very common. Under the Trump administration, this policy was hastily revoked,[47] with the OCR detailing new and burdensome rules on sexual assault cases in over 2,000 pages of minutely detailed procedures.[48]

Neither the EEOC nor the OCR have done a great job of enforcement. They have also delegated the brunt of enforcement responsibility to employers and schools themselves. The result has been a swift expansion of human resources offices and roles intended to combat these problems, including through the investigation of such complaints. The EEOC notes that "a prompt, thorough and impartial investigation of internal discrimination complaints about disciplinary action and taking appropriate corrective measures when necessary may resolve problems and prevent them from happening again."[49] On learning about a complaint, the EEOC maintains, an employer has a duty to investigate "promptly and thoroughly."[50] The Obama administration's changes to Title IX required schools that knew, or reasonably ought to know, that harassment was occurring to "take immediate action to eliminate the harassment, prevent its recurrence, and address its effects."[51]

The net result of these measures was a sharp rise in workplace investigations to fulfill these respective duties. The workplace investigation became the main tool to fulfill the substantive obligations to create a safe, healthy, as well as discrimination- and harassment-free workplace. Beginning around the time OSHA was passed, workplace investigations started to rise precipitously in mention in literature. A Google Ngram review shows the mention of "workplace investigations" over the last two hundred years across its corpus of printed sources (note the rise after the introduction of OSHA):[52]

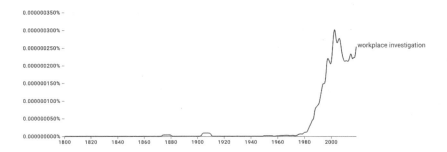

In the early days, many employers did a poor job of executing their obligations with workplace investigations. They conducted sloppy investigations.

Take the case of Patricia Fuller. In 1986, Fuller, a police officer for the city of Oakland, ended a three-year romantic relationship with her colleague, Antonio Romero. After breaking up with Romero, Fuller began receiving up to twenty-five "hang-up" calls a day, and only on her days off.[53] Even after she changed her number, she continued to receive these calls. When she changed her number a second time, Romero confronted her to demand why she had done so. In July 1987, Romero sped toward her in an unmarked police car, forcing her to swerve off the road to avoid a head-on collision.[54]

Despite all this conduct, Romero was promoted to a supervisory role over Fuller. Following continued harassment, other officers brought a complaint against Romero to an internal oversight body within the Oakland police force. Fuller requested that it not proceed since she was worried about her safety in light of Romero's drinking habits and his stated threats of suicide.

Nevertheless, she cooperated with the investigation; Romero did not. When Fuller was offered a transfer, she refused. Only when the oversight body closed the investigation and exonerated Romero, after it had not even interviewed him, did Fuller file a complaint under Title VII for discrimination on the basis of sex.

Bad investigations like this one became opportunities for courts to identify better standards around the duty to investigate, in effect taking the vague duties of statutes and articulating them for employers. In this case, the Oakland police force was heavily criticized for failing to exercise reasonable care in its investigation.

To take another example, in August 1985, Church's Fried Chicken, a fast-food franchise chain selling fried chicken, received sexual harassment and national origin discrimination complaints against a manager at one of its stores in Texas. How did they respond to the complaint? The franchise's headquarters sent the complaint to the accused manager himself to investigate, "like the fox in the proverbial chicken coop," a trial judge would later say.[55] Unsurprisingly, the manager's investigation into his own conduct was swift and exculpatory. His investigation found an El Salvadoran migrant worker employed at a *different* location—and who could not have committed the harm, on the face of the complaint itself—to be the offender.[56] On this pretext, he was fired.[57] It was a bad investigation, and, yet again, the court interceded to address the many procedural shortcomings.

But courts did not just supervise the quality of bad investigations. They began to use the carrot and the stick by recognizing that employers seeking to defend themselves from liability for the actions of bad employees could use workplace investigations to do so. In the landmark case of *Faragher v. City of Boca Raton*, the Supreme Court of the United States addressed the question of whether the city of Boca Raton would be liable for sexual harassment for the conduct of its municipal beach supervisors, one of whom had said to a female lifeguard employee: "Date me or clean the toilets for a year."[58] Noting the City "had entirely failed to disseminate its sexual harassment policy among the beach employees and that its officials made no attempt to keep track of the conduct of supervisors," the city was found responsible for the supervisors' conduct.[59] Nevertheless, the Supreme Court noted that an employer's reasonable efforts to stop the conduct, such as with a workplace investigation in response to a complaint, would have been a way of avoiding liability.

In *Burlington Industries, Inc v. Ellerth*, which was handed down the same day as Faragher, the Supreme Court found Kimberly Ellerth had been subjected to sexual harassment by her boss, who had invited her to a hotel lounge during a business trip and told her: "[Y]ou know, Kim, I could make your life very hard or very easy at Burlington."[60] In another instance, he told her: "[A]re you wearing shorter skirts yet, Kim, because it would make your job a whole heck of a lot easier."[61] The Supreme Court's decision was the same. While it found liability in this case, the court stated that taking actions to weed out such conduct, such as investigating complaints and taking action, would avoid liability.

Employers took note. Over the next two decades, they began to use workplace investigations to protect themselves from liability when employees sued them for discrimination or harassment perpetuated by their managers and coworkers. Today, the "Faragher-Ellerth Defense" helps employers avoid liability by exercising such reasonable care. It is responsible for the many policies, trainings, workplace investigations, and other devices that employers use to inculcate in their employees awareness of their legal obligations pertaining to discrimination and harassment.

While these measures serve to educate and modify behavior, their main goal is clear: to defend employers when employees sue them for allowing the conduct to occur. This might explain why these practices often feel insincere and shallow. It also explains, in part, why obtaining and performing a job is a greater exercise in bureaucracy than ever before. Employers are trying to avoid liability. (In the Cuomo investigation, one of Cuomo's accusers sued the state of New York in March 2023 for allowing the conduct to occur; it is almost certain that the state will point to its various policies, trainings, and the workplace investigation it conducted in its defense.)[62]

The courts have even gone a step further. They have made it clear that employers do not even need to know *with certainty* that bad conduct is happening; all they need is to notice it *might* be happening. In *Cotran v. Rollins Hudig Internat*, two women reported to their head of human resources that a director, Ralph Cotran, had harassed them when he had "exposed himself and masturbated in their presence."[63] Following an investigation that sustained their allegations, Cotran was fired.[64] He sued the employer. At trial, he produced evidence demonstrating that he had slept with both complainants in consensual sexual relationships. The jury found in his favor and returned a special verdict that Cotran had not engaged in the alleged conduct. On appeal, the court noted the real issue was whether the employer made the right move in investigating the allegations and acting to prevent harassment.[65] As long as a reasonable investigation concluded the conduct was happening, this was enough, even if a more fulsome investigation would have proven the conduct had not happened or did not meet the legal definition of harassment. Cotran's appeal was dismissed.

The consequences of structuring responsibility in this way are a subject of great debate in legal circles. Professor Eugene Volokh, an expert on the First Amendment in the United States, has argued that although courts rarely talk about discrimination and harassment laws in the context of free speech (statutes like Title VII only talk about "terms, conditions, or privileges of employment"),[66] they nevertheless restrain speech and conduct by indirect means because they penalize employers who fail to restrict the speech and conduct of their employees. The government threatens to punish the employer if the employer does not punish the employee.

The potential chilling effects are obvious. "[T]o be safe," writes Volokh, "an employer must suppress speech that *might* qualify as severe and pervasive enough to constitute harassment, even though, if litigated, the speech might not meet the legal standard. And this chilling effect is compounded by the fact . . . that employers derive no benefit from their employees' offensive speech, but must bear liability for it; this gives employers a great incentive to suppress even borderline speech."[67] A recent wide-ranging study of workplace investigations in Norway also noted that "the method of workplace investigations limits freedom of speech in the workplace, deteriorates the psychosocial work environment, and undermines the social partners' trust cooperation."[68]

The result is the fostering of an environment where employers are not encouraged to wait for complaints that would meet the rigorous standards of formal justice settings. Instead, they should act informally and fast. Fully fleshed-out complaints are not needed to start an investigation. Anonymous complaints are permissible. Sometimes, they are encouraged. Complainants may also be able to insist on requests to have workplace investigators of a certain background, such as a specific gender or race—something that would never happen in court.

Despite these critiques, there are obvious reasons why it *should* be the employer's responsibility to investigate complaints in health, safety, and discrimination and harassment. In nearly all cases, there is a clear power imbalance between what the employer and employee can do to exert control in the workplace. Even so, the contrast with liability in so many other contexts, where it is on the party experiencing injustice to enforce their rights and the offending party engaging in the alleged conduct to carry the risk of action, is striking. In our workplaces, we have made a choice. We have made employers the "frontline enforcers."[69]

Despite this history, it remains lost on many where the duty to investigate comes from. This explains why workplace investigations are so often unsatisfying for the parties involved.

While the downstream effect of workplace investigations is to make work environments healthy, safe, as well as discrimination- and harassment-free, these benefits are subservient to the main reason employers use them: to avoid liability. Because workplace investigations serve the employer's interests, the employer makes many critical decisions before, during, and after an investigation. This dynamic is akin to a situation where the person making treatment decisions is not the patient but the party paying for the care, who faces a penalty if they fail to exercise reasonable decision-making. No matter how empathetic they are, and regardless of the level of care or attention offered, the person making the final decisions is still not the patient receiving the actual treatment. They have their own bottom line.

Understanding this truth is not always easy for employees to accept. As many complainants learn, once a complaint is registered, it ceases to belong to them; it becomes the employer's responsibility. Indeed, the employer's feelings toward such a party are often characterized by more fear than sympathy, since the requirement to investigate is, in many cases, the employer's best defense against subsequent legal claims against the employer from the complainant himself or herself.[70] While the employer might respect or accommodate certain requests from a complainant, the employer will exert almost complete control over other aspects of the investigation, including deciding its scope. This loss of control happens early.

What is unfortunate about this dynamic is that, quite often, a complainant simply needs empathy more than anything else. In many situations, complainants' problems in the workplace may stem from a conflict in their work that does not go to issues of health, safety, discrimination, or harassment. It might relate to a personal or interpersonal malaise. But if the only outlets that allow the employee to be heard require casting the complaint in the language of health, safety, discrimination, or harassment, the employee will channel their complaints in the ways they must. Worse yet, complainants forced to adopt the language and framing they do not want—for example, labeling discomfort as harm just to be heard and referring to anxiety as discrimination just to get a response—would not only be contorting themselves for the system, but they would be misusing language in a way that causes many to see them as crying wolf. This subjects them to power systems that are not interested in solving their real problems. "The master's tools will never dismantle the master's house," as Audre Lorde once said.

* * *

Given the importance of work in people's lives, including as a source of identity and the main way they spend their time, many have also lost clarity that the basis of the employer–employee relationship is just a contract. Many people blur the lines at work between their workplace and their private lives.

Nothing illustrates this fact better than the way work provides many of us with our most important relationships. Many adults make most of their friends in the workplace. Indeed, 70 percent of employees affirm that having friends at work is the most important element of being happy at work.[71] Given that most people spend up to a third of their lives at work, it is also unsurprising that it has traditionally been common to meet romantic or sexual partners in these places. As recently as 2019, a third of Canadians admitted they had been in a romantic or sexual relationship with someone at work.[72] My own parents met in their workplace. Many famous couples met at work, including in relationships characterized by an uneven power dynamic. Michelle Robinson was Barack Obama's mentor at Sidley Austin LLP in 1989 when they began dating.[73]

Countless love stories have been written on these themes, too. One of the great love stories of the twentieth century, "The Bear Who Came Over the Mountain," by Alice Munro, which appeared in the *New Yorker* in 1999, is about a couple that began as a professor–student relationship.[74] *The Globe and Mail* newspaper columnist Doug Saunders wrote in the pages of that paper that his workplace romance turned marriage with fellow arts reporter Elizabeth Renzetti "saved my life."[75] In Renzetti's own "elegy for the office romance," she wrote: "I can't say I ever read [*The Globe and Mail*'s] Code of Conduct to find out whether my relationship with Doug contravened some *Globe* edict. I just assumed someone would tell me if I was in trouble."[76]

Renzetti's comment reveals how, for many, workplace romances are still perfectly acceptable unless they involve a power dynamic. But today, even neutral couplings are increasingly fraught. Some now maintain that any position with any semblance of power at work makes consent to a romantic or sexual relationship "truly impossible."[77] McDonald's CEO Steve Easterbrook was ousted from his role after his consensual office romance with an employee became known.[78] The relationship between CNN CEO Jeff Zucker's and chief marketing officer Allison Gollust, which was uncovered inadvertently as part of a separate workplace investigation and which both affirmed was consensual, resulted in both of them stepping down.[79] The top hourly billing rate of the firm conducting the workplace investigation was reportedly $2,000 per hour.[80]

With even consensual relationships now attracting this kind of punishment, there is significant confusion around what kind of personal relationships can be formed in the workplace. Recent polls show that two-thirds of American employees believe it necessary to "take extra caution around members of the opposite sex" in the workplace.[81] Studies consistently now show that increasing proportions of men altogether avoid one-on-one meetings with female co-workers (27 percent) or are reluctant to hire women for a job that would require close interaction (21 percent). In 2017, approximately a quarter of American men below the age of thirty stated they believed that asking a woman who is not a romantic partner to go for a drink was sexual harassment. The question was not limited to the workplace.[82] Many see no harm and only benefit in these statistics, but as someone who teaches at a university and watches how community members now significantly curtail and limit their exposure to one another, I see adverse effects on other possibilities of socialization and interaction.

Sociologically, these changes have transformed the workplace. As Eva Illouz notes, much of the recent change has focused on "instilling emotional self-regulation so as to remove the possibility of discomfort in another person."[83] While efforts, in particular, to protect women from abuses of institutional power by men are important, they have been achieved, writes Illouz, at the cost of "making the rules of fairness in the workplace trump the private desires of individuals."[84] Emotionally self-regulating workers are now encouraged to foster de-eroticized and de-sexualized workplaces, an odd contrast with the modern workplace obsession of encouraging workers to celebrate their sexual and gender expressions openly.

A workplace increasingly devoid of emotion also contrasts with the entertainment that many people consume. For example, Pornhub, the fourth most-visited website in the United States,[85] presents among its most-viewed videos many highly popular offerings set in the workplace.[86] The nine-season love story arch of Pam Beesly and Jim Halpert on *The Office* was a mythic workplace romance that gave birth to the trope of looking for "the Pam to my Jim" or "the Jim to my Pam," which, for a time, was a common trope on heterosexual dating apps.[87] As porn and television titillate viewers with motifs of workplace sex and romance, emotional self-regulation in the workplace is being normalized and imposed in ways that encourage people not to form romantic or sexual relationships with people they meet at work. All these changes, Illouz writes, have the effect of rewriting and transforming intimate desire, increasingly "subsuming the erotic and romantic experience of love under systematic rules of conduct."[88]

This, of course, is great news for employers.

Employers are not interested in the nuance of human relationships in the workplace. They are interested in avoiding liability. This is why they so often turn to lawyers to do this work. For the most part, there are very few requirements in most jurisdictions as to who can conduct workplace investigations. While some jurisdictions require investigators to attain minimal thresholds of training,[89] most do not have any binding standards. For its part, the EEOC says an investigator "should be well-trained in the skills that are required for interviewing witnesses and evaluating credibility."[90] Several fair employment practices agencies have guidance mirroring this requirement.[91] Some jurisdictions require external, or third-party, investigators to be licensed.[92]

In practice, most employers prefer a lawyer. By entering a lawyer–client relationship, the workplace investigator's work is subject to privilege, which the employer can use to block disclosure of any investigative file or report, or they can waive privilege and disclose these materials, if they so wish.[93] Lawyers are also trained to see liabilities and, in doing so, to reduce disputes involving complex human experiences and emotions into abstract questions about responsibility. Just as courts "cast about for the right rule to apply, the most familiar box in which to cram the dispute, limbs and all," lawyer-investigators are excellent at sniffing for liability.[94] That is a function of their profession.

But there are many problems with this approach to resolving workplace conflicts. Everyone, not just lawyers, should be involved in maintaining a safe, healthy, and respectful workplace. When it comes to rights, we all have a role in recognizing and accommodating them—common sense over common law. This is something we have forgotten as we have delegated so much responsibility to employers to conduct workplace investigations and let them, in turn, use lawyers to confirm they are fulfilling their obligations. All too often, these devices neither aim to exercise common sense nor elevate the common good. They specifically take the conflict out of the hands of employees and put important decisions about fact-finding in the hands of a third party, crystallizing disputes between two individuals as a question of legal rights and wrongs, even if they do not come to legal findings. And it costs a lot of money.

This approach to the adjudication of employees' problems is one that too often leads to zero-sum battles and the creation of what Jamal Greene calls "rock-ribbed rights."[95] The vindication of an individual's rights through this system, however, is not the same as raising the working conditions of a collective. Indeed, the atomization of employees, where the only avenues of recourse and power are filing complaints against managers and coworkers premised on recognized rights to health, safety, and freedom from discrimination and harassment, presents a startling contrast from the era of collective employee power when unions were stronger.

Moreover, it speaks to a phenomenon that has taken root as the accountability of leaders becomes more difficult and income inequalities more rampant. In many respects, this only erodes possibilities for solidarity between workers, whose employment situations are already increasingly precarious. For employers, this is not a bad thing. Framing a dispute that stems from social or organizational issues or broader aspects of a toxic environment or job by focusing on the micro-context of conflicts between specific employees can help reinforce those very systems and structures.

In the United States, perhaps nothing epitomizes the limits of a legal system premised on vindicating individual rights to remediate collective harms than the experience of race. The legal categorization of people as property on the basis of a collective attribute, their skin color, petrified racial injustice into the country's origins. The notion that individual rights would serve as a viable vehicle of repair for these collective harms was always suspect. Thinking that a private employer can repair such deep-rooted harms displays either a resounding faith in proprietary justice or a blind eye to the scope of the challenge. For example, when a white reporter on ESPN was caught on video disparaging a Black colleague for getting increased airtime because of her skin color and because the channel was "feeling pressure" on diversity,[96] the ensuing workplace investigation became a meditation on race in America. In so many respects, the underlying issues are not those that a mere workplace investigation can resolve. And yet that is exactly what we ask it to do.

Complicating this trend is another hard truth. The duties to conduct workplace investigations in response to health, safety, discrimination, and harassment concerns have become more firmly recognized at precisely the same time that the language around health, safety, discrimination, and harassment has increasingly been shorn of their shared, uniform understandings. These terms might have narrow and specific legal meanings, but their broader meanings are political, cultural, and generational. They are often in debate.

Point in case. Despite the laudable achievements of health and safety legislation making our workplaces healthier and safer than ever before, even this statement of fact might be outright rejected by someone contesting my implicit view of what constitutes health and safety, in particular because of my focus on physical health and safety. In recent years, many people have come to have different understandings of harm and violence. The same is also true of discrimination and harassment.

Among my own generation (I was born in 1987), there has been a sharp rise in the phenomenon of "therapy-speak" that prioritizes revelation and sharing of traumatic experiences. Candor about difficult experiences is a point of pride for many. But having conversations with someone about events that are perceived, felt, and interpreted with the force of trauma makes it difficult to treat or talk about those events with objectivity, which is supposed to be the point of a workplace investigation. This makes it very hard to treat something as objectively minor when it does not feel that way. The tenor of truth has become different for everyone in ways that are tantamount to physical battles. "When people don't want to participate in a conversation any longer, they say they're 'tapping out' like in wrestling," observes comedian Steven Phillips-Horst. "I recently heard 'Save my bullets' to refer to not asking someone to do something. It's like we're yearning for something physical and heroic in the realm of the neutered, the digital, the mundane."[97]

This might not be a problem, except that when these issues flare up in a workplace, we often forget how ill-suited workplace investigations are for having conversations where we might not be able to agree on the base terms of discussion. Words and experiences touch people in different ways. One's description of violence might feel overstated to another. One's off-the-cuff remark might sear into another's memory, while a deeply considered comment intended to create lasting impact might leave none at all. Taking these experiences and then invoking and wrapping them in a rights discourse can occlude the fact that what is really needed is just a plain, open discussion, the equivalent of taking a heated X conversation offline to get a cup of coffee.[98] But such conversations are getting harder and harder to have.

On top of all of this, the changing nature and porosity of today's communications make it easier than ever to misunderstand *and* report on one another. To be sure, this environment has created new forms of age-old harassment, as an Alaska employer found out when they had to investigate one employee who wrote to his female colleague before a weekend: "Good to know you're almost done with the project and headed for the weekend. Do you garden? ⬎"[99] But in less gray cases, and much of where workplace investigators operate is gray, communication can be subject to misinterpretation and miscommunication. And those contexts are endless, as boundaries between the public and private dissipate. We live in an age, as Phillips-Horst jokingly puts it, "when everyone is a whistleblower—when people post screengrabs of interoffice Slack drama to X seconds after their co-worker misgenders an M&M."[100]

CHAPTER THREE

MAGIC WORDS

A few years ago, I was attending the American Bar Association's Labor and Employment Law's Annual Section Conference in San Francisco. The event is an annual gathering of hundreds of top lawyers representing employees, employers, unions, and government agencies, as well as neutral investigators, in-house counsel, and academics, with parallel tracks of seminars on just about every employment law topic one can imagine. For employment law nerds, the conference is paradise.

During the proceedings, I chatted with one workplace investigator at the fringes of a large conference room about a recent matter the investigator was working on. It featured a very difficult complainant who consistently found fault in the conduct and actions of others and never in himself.

"This employee just can't get along in the sandbox with anyone else in his department," said the investigator. "If you ask everyone else, the problem is him; everyone corroborates that. But if you ask him, it's like a parallel universe. His take is that no one should be able to tell him what to do. When anyone critiques him, it's abuse. When people say nice things about other people, it is somehow a slight against him."

"What is the investigation about, exactly?" I asked.

"Does it even matter?" said the lawyer, throwing up their hands in a gesture of resignation. "He uses magic words. He knows exactly how to use them, too. He has a journal of all these little events and moments, in crazy detail. Every action is discrimination based on this or that protected characteristic, or retaliation for engaging in protected activity because he complains about unsafe practices in the workplace."

I nodded, because I, too, was aware of this phenomenon. There are many valid complaints and many complainants who are the victims of injustice who deserve to be heard but never are—often because their complaints are never filed. A recent EEOC study found 70 percent of victims of harassment—to name but one type of complaint—never raise an internal complaint, with only 6 percent to 13 percent of victims making one formally.[1] These numbers are shockingly low.

But frivolous complainants are a different story. They speak to a different problem that the world of workplace investigations has created: one where parties fluent in "magic words" can assure they will be heard, often regardless of the dictates of common sense. These magic words serve as on-switches in the legal system. They activate an employers' concern about the legal obligations identified in the previous chapter.

In most common law legal systems of tort liability, it is already a well-accepted truth that the party who suffers the loudest will get the most attention. The squeaky wheel gets the grease. Like in personal injury claims, the party who shrieks over even the most mundane injury, such as the person who buys and spills on themselves an obviously hot cup of coffee, might receive the biggest payout. By contrast, those who suffer in silence will not be entitled to the same type of relief.

This system, for better or worse, incentivizes and rewards complaints. Unlike in cultures where the nail that sticks out gets hammered back in, many common law countries have created a series of implicit rewards for complaining. A complaint may serve to inoculate an individual from an adverse action, like being fired for incompetence, since employers wary of claims of retaliation will avoid firing complaining employees for fear of retaliating against them. This system presents a clear benefit to employees who record and document *any* type of behavior or conduct that might give rise to a complaint, so that they can use a complaint as future insurance. Seeking a departure, it can be a way to get a payout, and if the costs of that payout are lower than the costs of a workplace investigation or lawsuit, doesn't it make sense to just pay it?

Complaining can be a way to achieve ends. Any information that puts an employer on notice of liability creates an incentive to conduct a workplace investigation. So how do employers balance that obligation with the willingness of a bad faith employee to seize those terms to lodge complaints that do not merit attention, such as to avoid any merely unwanted interaction at all, even when it may be a necessary part of one's job, such as a regular performance review or providing feedback?

Workplace investigations, in many cases, are simply not what are needed to improve the workplace. But what other tools do we have? Often enough, a conflict situation between two people that could have been resolved by other means, like a difficult conversation that draws out and reveals the complexity of the actors involved to each other, is replaced by a proprietary device that involves lawyers and no direct conversation between the parties at all, as the adjudication runs its course. While certainly not true in all cases, it is often the equivalent of going to the emergency room for an ailment that never merited it. Introducing a lawyer-investigator into a workplace can have the effect of heightening tensions rather than achieving resolution.

American writer Sarah Schulman has written about the inflation of disagreement, discord, and conflict with escalated terms like abuse. As she noted in *Conflict Is Not Abuse*, escalating conflict into harm, casting mere discord or discomfort as harmful to one's safety, has become a common way to avoid accountability. Abusers externalize blame. To them, it is *always* someone else's fault. How, then, do we reconcile this observation with the receptive devices we have created to listen to those who are victims of unhealthy, unsafe, discriminatory, or harassing workplaces? How do we stop people from misusing these systems by assuming the victim's voice specifically to mete out harm on the target of their accusations? As Schulman writes, we live with this paradigm because a thinking has set in that "if you are not in an abusive relationship, you don't deserve help. Being 'abused' is what makes you 'eligible' for help."[2] And yet, as she notes, "everyone deserves help and compassion."[3]

Schulman takes this position after observing how inaccurate claims of abuse are so often intended to express shunning and punishment or as ways of exonerating terrible acts. In one of her most potent examples, she examines how police brutality against racialized people is often justified by unwarranted assertions of threat. Rather than account for internalized or systemic racism, allegations of harm escalate the discourse and exonerate awful behavior, including violence itself. Her experience as an activist during the HIV/AIDS pandemic in the 1980s and 1990s taught her the sanctions of shunning and punishment do not resolve conflict in relationships. Contact, she writes, is what improves relationships. Schulman recognizes that "it is a community around a conflict that is the source of its resolution."[4]

Yet complaining is often readily encouraged. As Schulman describes in her work, upon discovering that a graduate student of hers had been writing about her on a blog, and engaging in behavior that some may have characterized as unwanted stalking or harassment, she was encouraged by coworkers to report the individual to an authority. She did not do so. Instead, she spoke directly with the student and engaged in a difficult but useful conversation to obtain resolution. This experience is described at length in her work to prove her assertion that contact and community are the sources of resolution.

Although Schulman is right, contact is far from the first choice when employees have problems with one another. Lodging complaints and requesting workplace investigations is a way of limiting contact, since concerns about retaliation often cause already tense relationships to either cease altogether or turn into sterile relationships. A lack of contact is encouraged. Until workplace investigations conclude, allegations that have been neither sustained nor rejected are in a kind of abeyance of truth. This might last for years. As this occurs, a new reality solidifies where there is often no communication between the parties. If the workplace relationship is unavoidable, such as an investigation involving two co-workers or a manager and one of their direct reports, the relationship often moves toward documented, unidirectional communication like email. Such formats are not conducive to repairing communication. When relayed back to our allies and friends, stories of victimization or one's negative experiences receiving these communications can easily reinforce narratives of victimhood, inflate conflict, and result in overstating harm.

Although Schulman does not write about the world of workplace investigations directly, her observations about the desire for shunning go straight to one of their central problems. By responding to complaints from an employee formulated within the tight categories of liability, workplace investigations become decisions about the truth that will impact people's employment. Often, those adjudications have stakes that go to punishment, since employees found to have engaged in certain conduct might be subject to adverse employment actions, like termination. The entire structure of the investigation, starting with the complaint, is intended to force a respondent to reckon with the reality of the complainant, one that carries a potential result of sanction and punishment. This is why Schulman's distinction between conflict and abuse in these situations is important. While workplace investigations identifying and attributing responsibility for *abuse* are just, "in situations of *conflict*, accusations that attribute sole responsibility to one party and then construct them as deserving of punishment and shunning are *unjust* [emphasis added]." The misappropriation of complaint systems by non-deserving actors is one of the reasons why Shulman believes it is so important to separate overstated harm from real harm—"to retain the legitimate protections and recognitions afforded the experience of actual violence and oppression."[5]

It is an unfortunate truth that many investigations are born from mere anxiety and discomfort. How we tackle these cognitive distortions is a challenging question. "At many levels of human interaction," writes Shulman, "there is the opportunity to conflate discomfort with threat, to mistake internal anxiety for exterior anger, and, in turn, to escalate rather than resolve." Seeing ourselves as transgressed becomes a quick way to explain difficult experiences, as well as to avoid self-accountability. I have seen this underlying dynamic, a situation in which the respondent becomes a "receptacle of anxieties"[6] for the complainant, repeat itself many times. These cognitive distortions are part of life. We blame people for things that come from inside us. We hasten to critique the behavior of others we see in ourselves. And often, we do not always know how we feel or why we feel the way we do. Blame is a useful tactic.

This is to say nothing of the immense pressure on the parties themselves. Complainants often pay dire consequences for coming forward. One academic study of 683,419 complaints about discrimination filed with the EEOC between 2012 and 2016 noted that 63 percent of parties eventually lost their job, with negotiated or mandated change in only 7 percent of cases and a median payout of just $8,500 for the complainant.[7] A private survey by HRAcuity of employer data showed that, in 2022, 40 percent of sexual harassment allegations were substantiated while 45 percent were not, and 69 percent of disability discrimination claims and 74 percent of retaliation claims were not substantiated. Respondents, of course, deal with career suicide and sometimes worse. In the United Kingdom, the General Medical Council, the regulatory body that is responsible for investigating doctors accused of professional wrongdoing, has released statistics on its own investigations that show that a third of doctors investigated by the regulatory body have suicidal thoughts as investigations take place. (Investigations sometimes take years.) Shockingly, 3 percent of doctors investigated by the body commit suicide.[8]

While Schulman rightly notes that these processes often lead towards shunning and punishment, Ian Buruma has proffered another interesting hypothesis. Buruma was famously exited from the *New York Review of Books* for the act of publishing "a controversial piece by a controversial figure," an article by Jian Ghomeshi that now contains a 207-word explanatory note on the *Review*'s site stating that "more than twenty women accused [Ghomeshi] of sexual abuse and harassment, which included hitting, biting, choking, and verbal abuse during sex."[9] In a reflective piece in *Harper's*, Buruma likens expressions of contrition, apology, and wrongdoing to "the Protestant goal of ethical perfection," in which modern-day heirs of the this ethic obtain and express status "by having the right opinions on social and cultural issues."[10] As Buruma notes:

> It has become almost mandatory, for example, for Fortune 500 companies to publish a Diversity, Equity, and Inclusion (DEI) statement that swears allegiance to the right values, regardless of how divorced those values are from what the company does. "We are on a journey from awareness to commitment to action" (PepsiCo, Inc.); "Diversity and inclusion are the foundation of our culture, and reflect our values of doing what's right" (Lockheed Martin); "We have long been committed to promoting inclusion, diversity, and equity" (Goldman Sachs).[11]

What matters in these announcements is not their substance so much as their public aspect and their deployment of skepticism-prohibiting dogma. Moreover, this public quality of the allegiance to virtue and repentance of any past harm stands in as a replacement for any attempt to address issues with "serious and systematic reform."[12] Just as knowing how to use the right opinions, values, and language serves to assert ethical superiority in the public sphere, in the intimate environment of the workplace, these dynamics also determine who gets to complain. Like elsewhere in the justice system, questions of power are inseverable from whose complaints get heard. As Schulman's observations suggest, a heightened rhetoric of harm does little to elevate the complaints of people who experience real harm. "People from privileged groups, or who overlap with the groups society is designed to serve," she writes, "have expectations that their complaint will be heard. Obviously, white and bourgeois people are more likely to have their accusations taken seriously."[13]

History can show countless examples of that. Many of the pivotal cases in the history of Title IX, which prohibits sex-based discrimination in schools and institutions receiving federal grants, come from Yale University, an institution that is synonymous with elite privilege. Following a series of test cases in the mid-1970s emanating from Yale University, a federal judge made the landmark determination that Title IX included quid pro quo sexual harassment because "academic advancement conditioned upon submission to sexual demands constitutes sexual discrimination in education." This finding constituted a major expansion of the meaning of Title IX, and many universities established formal grievance procedures and policies with which many are familiar today. Yale University goes on to play another key role in the evolution of Title IX, when Yale student Alexandra Brodsky founded the Know Your IX group that sought to impose more obligations on schools to combat sexual assault (and to push back against referring such cases to law enforcement). The Yale-centeredness of the history of Title IX reflects the significant fact that several of the key figures in the history of Title IX have been members of the most advantaged classes of American society.

This should not be surprising. "Power," writes Sara Ahmed, who resigned in 2016 from Goldsmiths, a constituent research university of the University of London, in an act of protest against the institution's culture of sexual harassment, "is not simply what complaints are about; power shapes what happens when you complain."[14] These dynamics are important because they speak to a core reason why the complainant loses so much agency in the telling of their complaint. The employer's concern for the complaint is premised on the fear of liability. It is this concern, not charity or empathy for the complainant, that is the main catalyst for a workplace investigation. Because of that, a complaint may be reshaped and tweaked to address how the employer feels they are exposed to liability. Although complainants are often depicted as parties that should be empowered by the process, empowerment is not what most employers are trying to provide.

Sometimes, it should be. In my own investigations, the most important task is just listening to the complainant. Once I have mapped the nature of the complaint and examined the structure of a workplace (and any relevant written evidence), I usually schedule a long interview with the complainant. I try to impose almost no constraints on this interview. If there is a written complaint, I ask the complainant, line by line, about their allegations. The effect is almost always the same. Complainants feel empowered at having the chance to share their experiences. For many, the effect of this empowerment is deeply cathartic. For some, it can even provide all the resolution they seek from the process of making a complaint—getting the opportunity to be heard. But regardless of how the complainant feels, the process rarely stops there. I am not a therapist. Empowerment is not the goal of a workplace investigation. The complaint is no longer in their hands. If the complaint raises claims susceptible to attracting liability, an employer, indeed, must continue the process regardless of how the complainant feels. It is a perfect example of how the "rigidity of legal dictates precludes the exercise of judgment."[15] As many complainants find out, a workplace investigation takes on a life of its own.

It is often only at this stage that many complainants learn that workplace investigations were developed to protect employers themselves. Protecting complainants is only a byproduct of this mission. As Ahmed recently told *The Paris Review*, complaints are where one goes to "hear and learn about institutional mechanics, how institutions reproduce themselves."[16] Naturally, many complainants do not know how to navigate these systems. As she writes: "If you can't locate the procedure, you do not know how to proceed."[17] But the corollary is also true: complainants who know the procedures all too well are capable of weaponizing those procedures to further their worthless complaints. Those who have the master's tools will always be able to wield them in desirable ways.

The challenge of legal orders intended to empower victims by protecting individuals when it comes to health and safety, as well as on the basis of certain protected characteristics, has to grapple with this reality. Like any system, it has created and enshrined new elites fluent in these enumerated rights and categories, or otherwise protected by their membership in certain systems. This dynamic creates and perpetuates power.[18] For an example of this phenomenon, look at Stanford University's "Protected Identity Harm Reporting" system, which permits reporting "community member experiences of harm," but only if you are a member of Stanford's community.[19] The mechanism specifically removes the power of complaining from people who are not Stanford University students or employees, such as the many homeless people living in their vehicles along El Camino Real, only steps away at the fringes of campus.

Politics is a significant part of the problem, too. Many of the questions we ask workplace investigations to address are really about disputes driven by disagreements in values and normative views. And how we decide these questions often comes down to politics.

Just look at how unsuccessful we are in keeping politicians accountable. In 2014, Justin Trudeau summarily suspended two male backbench MPs from his caucus for facing mere accusations of misconduct in their treatment of two female colleagues, with no investigation whatsoever,[20] and even though Trudeau himself had similarly faced a mere accusation without any similar consequences.[21] Likewise, President Trump suspended White House Communications Director Anthony Scaramucci after only ten days on the job for telling a reporter, "I'm not trying to suck my own cock," even though the president had actually been recorded saying objectively far worse things.[22] The politics of the workplace have become fierce battles of accountability, even as the conduct of our political leaders has become less so. Workplace investigations have intensified conflict at the scale of many immediate and intimate work relationships, even while those who possess real power are seemingly inoculated from similar types of accountability. The fact that a Canadian prime minister or an American president can get away with behavior that an average citizen would not speak to a familiar dynamic of power and accountability. It also suggests the battles many might be fighting in the workplace are political, not legal, ones.

Research backs this up. Surveys demonstrate that people are more likely to report certain conduct giving rise to a workplace investigation, and to view workplace investigations as legitimate, based on their political leanings. Democrats are more likely to report harassment.[23] Republicans are less likely to consider online harassment a major problem.[24] In a poll conducted after the election of President Trump, 62 percent of Democrats stated they believed "men getting away with sexual harassment or assault is a major problem."[25] By contrast, only 33 percent of Republicans felt the same way.[26] This was around the same time that three-quarters of all Republicans attested to the #MeToo movement having gone too far, when only a quarter of Democrats agreed with that same statement.[27] Unfortunately, workplace investigations cannot resolve these substantive debates. It is a problem when we cannot agree on base terms.

This phenomenon affects not only the likelihood a complaint will be sustained or the number of complaints filed but also the *type* of complaints that are filed. Studies show that conservatives are less likely to report experiencing sexual harassment.[28] By contrast, they are *more* likely to report non-physically aggressive forms of harassment, such as those related to political identity.[29] According to a study from 2020, 77 percent of "staunch conservatives" attested to not feeling confident they could say what they believe (the number was 42 percent among liberals).[30] No wonder twenty-one states have pushed for the passage of bills prohibiting the teaching of "divisive concepts" (and, ironically, often setting out draconian procedures for their investigation).[31] Those who lean liberal are more likely to consider ambiguous conduct in the workplace as sexual harassment, and to report it as such, than those who lean conservative.[32] Those who lean liberal are far more likely to find certain jokes or comments constituting sexual harassment.[33]

A poll by Ipsos/NPR found that "partisanship is the biggest driver of differences" in beliefs regarding sexual assault and sexual harassment, not gender or sex.[34] The Republican–Democrat split in agreement with the statement "[f]alse accusations of sexual harassment against men are very common" is 73 percent Republican against 36 percent of Democrats. The political split in this poll was more significant than any other divide along demographic or characteristic lines. No wonder political affiliation has become important in romantic rituals. Nowadays, 86 percent of Americans think it is harder to date someone without the same political leanings.[35]

Of course, imbalances in who complains are not necessarily new in other respects. For example, only 17 percent of EEOC complaints tend to be brought by men. But the political character of our differences has fundamentally affected the legitimacy of workplace investigations themselves. This, in a nutshell, is one of the major problems we face when turning to them to solve conflict. Those who lean liberal are much more likely to see the workplace investigation as a legitimate instrument of justice. Those who lean conservative are not. Given this difference, use of the device may only serve to reenforce the positions of both camps. The device then risks becoming an instrument of power, not justice.

"The purpose of politics is to negotiate over disagreement," writes Jamal Greene. "The purpose of law is to set the ground rules for that negotiation."[36] The workplace investigation is not a space for negotiated disagreement. It is a space to make findings about disputed facts. When political disputes undermine the procedure of an investigation itself, those findings become less legitimate. The workplace investigation then turns into a device to confirm one's views. Invocations of legally charged and conclusive language, which is at the core of what employers really want to investigate to avoid liability, make it impossible to listen. This has a deleterious effect when, quite often, the best way to resolve conflict is to drop all conclusive language and engage with the other in all their complexity, rather than the labels. Engaging with someone in this way is inherently respectful. It treats another's viewpoint as complex and real.

No matter how much we revere and respect procedure, this will not address substantive dispute over fundamental understandings, which are often at issue in workplace investigations. Perhaps nothing better illustrates this reality than new trends in self-identification, which have only further muddied the waters of the duty to investigate.

Self-identification is hardly new when it comes to equality issues in the workplace. In the United States, asking employees to self-identify certain characteristics such as their race, ethnicity, and sex is commonplace; indeed, the Civil Rights Act of 1964 requires employers to report this information to the federal government.[37] Self-identification surveys are the main ways employers fulfill these obligations. Responding to contemporary imperatives of equality, many employers have also broadened the scope of identities to which employees can self-disclose.[38] Self-identification in these contexts is largely a question of expediency and trust. But it is also prone to misrepresentative and bad faith claims, since it is possible to self-identify to a false identity in such systems, too.

In this respect, self-identification gives rise to some very difficult questions, especially when it comes to assertions of belonging and membership to groups in ways that others do not or refuse to recognize. Claims or assertions of certain identities, especially those where identity markers are associated with certain features, characteristics, or behaviors that do not appear to be present to another person, have become cultural flashpoints today. Such disputes have become even more complicated by the fact that self-identification often occurs *in* oppressed groups, not power-holding ones. Unlike solidarity and allyship, this phenomenon of self-identification results in actively assuming the status of oppressed identities, often creating entitlements to rights or protections. In such situations, whether someone is willing to take another person at their word that the person is the identity they affirm, rather than upon verification, certification, or some other kind of proof, goes fundamentally to questions of trust. Whether that trust exists now poses important strains on, and difficult challenges to, existing legal regimes, especially those designed to create rights and entitlements or provide protections for equity-seeking groups that have been the subject of a historical, social, or other disadvantage. The erosion of trust presents significant challenges to the frameworks intended to achieve equality.

A few examples of these contemporary disputes may be in order. For example, many educational settings, like the university where I teach, have developed systems to certify disabilities and entitle students with disabilities to accommodations. Rather than focus on principles of universal design, this certification system allows students to avail themselves of accommodations like extra test-writing time or assistance in taking lecture notes. Demand for these accommodations has ballooned. Accessibility services at my university are now larger than the history and English departments combined. Many students who do not enjoy such accommodations feel resentment at those who have gained them or suspect they are misusing them to get unfair advantages. It is not naive to wonder if the "proliferation of administrators" engendered by this system has had any impact on the cost of post-secondary education,[39] which has risen at twice the rate of inflation over the last forty years.[40] But this is just the start of questions we might ask.

Questions of trust, sincerity, and verification are becoming apparent in many other contexts where self-identification issues are the centers of dispute. In Scotland, Scottish Prime Minister Nicola Sturgeon's gender recognition certificate bill, which would have simplified the legal process for people seeking to change their legal gender, recently contributed to bringing down her leadership,[41] at a time when self-identification has become a clarion call of the trans movement.[42] In Canada, false self-identification to claims of Indigeneity—especially by individuals gaining advantages from organizations seeking to bolster representation of Indigenous Peoples in accordance with legal requirements and the imperative of reconciliation between Indigenous and settler populations[43]—has led to headline-grabbing stories, including with individuals being dismissed from their positions, or asked to step down from them, or being stripped of honorary degrees and titles.[44] In the United States, self-identification issues plagued the presidential campaign of Elizabeth Warren. Elsewhere, stories of individuals being "unmasked" of the identities to which they have claimed membership feature regularly in the news.[45]

What are these disputes about? Are they about misrepresentation of the "truth"? This explanation would suggest that an objective fact is being undermined by a non-factual assertion of belonging and mem-bership. Such explanations are common in the context of squabbles over "immutable" identities.[46] Others suggest that they remain pinned to perennial forms of hate and phobia. Still another explanation is that they are fundamentally disputes about fairness, arising from outrage or frustration that rights, protections, or entitlements for the disadvantaged should not serve as incentives for those committing fraud to obtain (or weaponize) those rights, protections, or entitlements. This explanation is compelling in scenarios involving the awarding of a benefit to a group identity being claimed (e.g., advantage in hiring), which may be gained dishonestly.

Regardless of one's take, all these examples speak to a broader anxiety about the limits of self-identification in various modern contexts. While regimes that protect against discrimination and harassment are important gains from the civil rights movement, they did not anticipate the degree to which trends of self-identification would challenge the base presumptions of these frameworks. Identity categories themselves have become sites of debate. The system has neither changed nor kept up; the opposite is true. As one commentator dryly notes: "Even as many ordinary citizens think of identity in more fluid terms, elite institutions and new public policies are creating strong incentives for ordinary citizens to double down on their . . . identities."[47]

None of the above even begins to touch on the reality that our identities are also frequently, well, just messy. We cover or heighten our identities in specific situations for all kinds of reasons. In the faculty in which I teach, several straight male teachers organize a fantasy hockey pool league. Despite having a great-grandfather who was a famous hockey player, I do not ever watch hockey. I cannot even name five hockey teams. But I participate in the league, since it is an opportunity to interact with colleagues with whom I might otherwise not. In these interactions, as in many interactions with straight men, I find myself inadvertently engaging in acts of "covering" my gay identity.[48] I lower my voice. I uncross my legs. I change many of my cultural references. And yet, often only a short time later, if I find myself surrounded by my gay friends, it is common for me to *heighten* these same identity traits, raising my voice, crossing my legs, and even ironically exchanging epithets like "queer" and "faggot" that would be foul in the other context. To what extent are such fluctuations natural? And to what extent are the perceptions of my environment a motivation for me to engage in these behaviors? Is the hockey pool league not oppressive? Who is responsible for how I feel and the actions I take?

Do I not have the stirrings of a worthy complaint, if I wanted to file one?

CHAPTER FOUR

SCOPING

Once a complaint is shared and the employer decides to act, the investigation must be framed. This is the question of scope. Scoping an investigation is a deceptively simple but critical moment, possibly the most important moment, even though it precedes evidence gathering, credibility determinations, and fact-finding. It involves determinations about what allegations the investigator will examine and any resource constraints on their work. For example, will the investigator be paid to produce a full-blown investigative report containing all evidence, or will the employer save on costs by paying merely for a short, oral debrief? Determining such resource questions is the responsibility of the employer alone. More seasoned employers have some skill in anticipating these costs. Others, less so. In 2020, my hometown of Grimsby, Ontario, a small town near Toronto, was inflamed by a spate of complaints giving rise to workplace investigations that stemmed from some coarse interactions between elected town councilors. Although the town had budgeted $5,000 for the investigations, they ended up spending $72,926,[1] money that might have gone to something like the local library or summer jobs for students. In neighboring Niagara Falls, the municipality spent $270,000 on investigations from 2015 to 2020.[2]

Given the employer pays the investigator and is conscientious about costs, scoping is the area where the ethical tensions in the impartial and independent nature of a workplace investigator's job come most alive. The potential bias of an investigator who is paid by the employer is a source of suspicion for many in the process. How can an investigator, they ask, remain impartial? How can the investigator divorce their financial self-interest by not colluding with an employer to arrive at an outcome the employer might want (whether favorable to the complainant or respondent)? What kind of lawyer being paid by a client really is comfortable investigating or coming to findings that are inconvenient for their client? Who would really want to piss off a client in such a way? What about any future business with that client?

Such dynamics are not unlike regulatory watchdogs meant to police industry and government action. Just as workplace investigators are generally hired on a case-by-case basis, regulatory watchdogs often hold their positions through short-term and precarious appointments. "The terms are short," writes Ron Ellis in a stinging critique of the administrative state, *Unjust by Design*, "but appointees are routinely led to expect that when their current term expires, the government will appoint them for a further term, and then a further term, and so on. Governments do routinely reappoint members and chairs, but they may arbitrarily refuse reappointments and frequently do so."[3] This may happen when enforcers suddenly become serious about enforcement. The rule of law implications of this partisan patronage system, appointments-as-gifts, are obvious. "It is a culture," writes Ellis, "freighted with government expectations of a tie between the government and the recipient of the gift, a tie characterized by loyalty and acceptance of a shared agenda."[4] Courts have acknowledged these positions are "intrinsically precarious."[5] Besides questions of financial interest like those of appointment-holders, how can lawyers reconcile their professional duty to advance a client's interests while remaining objective as a factfinder? After all, the American Bar Association's Model Rules, which every state has used in some respect to design its ethical rules for attorneys, and which all American jurisdictions test on their respective bar exams, say that lawyers should "act with commitment and dedication to the interests of the client and with zeal in advocacy upon the client's behalf."[6]

This is an area where figures within the employment law bar on all sides of the debate have much to say. In a high-profile article recently disseminated to members of the California employment law bar, attorneys Andrew H. Friedman and Courtney Abrams rejected any assertion that workplace investigators can be impartial or independent. They argue that workplace investigations are "inherently structured to benefit the investigators' client employers from start to finish," since investigators have a financial incentive to structure investigations in a way employers want and to "defer to their client's wishes regarding not just the scope of the investigation, but also form of the investigatory report."[7] Moreover, a lawyer-investigator's duties to share information with the employer override any confidentiality they might be able to offer other parties in an investigation.[8]

How would attorney-investigators rebut these allegations? They would state that the duty of furthering their client's interests is not at all difficult to reconcile with their neutral work: an impartial investigation serves the employer by providing an objective telling of the facts. When it is not possible for employers themselves to conduct a workplace investigation, given conflicts of interest, the size of the workplace, or any other appearances of taint, impropriety, or bias, outsourcing it to a third party is an ideal way to accomplish this task. An employer-client, most workplace investigators would say, can use the investigative report to respond accordingly, such as by taking measures to train, coach, demote, or terminate an employee. The investigation would further the employer's interest by showing they took reasonable measures to gain an objective telling of the facts.

Moreover, attorney-investigators exclude themselves from the decision-making process that involves their investigation. This helps keep their interests separate from the client's. As I noted in the introduction, the final stage of a workplace investigation is submitting the report. Once submitted, there is no need to stay involved; the employer decides what to do with it. The reasons for this separation are clear. Remaining involved in any decision-making process afterward would risk tainting the fact-finding process itself, as the investigator might be tempted to collect and find certain information. Further, investigations can be and are often reviewed during litigation after the fact, a healthy check on the process. This way, courts can scrutinize the practices of investigators and establish standards and impose safeguards, practices that filter back into how investigations are conducted.

More difficult than the lawyer's execution of and respect for their ethical duties are the questions of power that attend to scoping the investigation. Scoping is essential to all investigations. Without a scope, there is no investigation. But the scope of an investigation is not a banal exercise. It is a question of resources, dictated by the employer paying for the process. It is not the investigator who makes these decisions and determines what will be investigated. This has a fundamental impact on the neutral work the workplace investigator ultimately does. One colleague once told me that workplace investigators are "truth advocates." The reality is that they are only allowed to advocate for the truth on the matters within the scope they have.

To understand why this issue is so important to the question of neutrality, imagine an investigator entering a workplace with two employees raising mutual allegations of misconduct against one another.

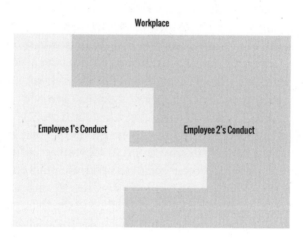

What is investigated in this workplace is the employer's choice. As the Association of Workplaces Investigators states unequivocally in its foundation document, *Guiding Principles for Investigators Conducting Impartial Workplace Investigations* (Guiding Principle #1): "An impartial workplace investigation should occur when an employer has determined that one is necessary." It is this determination, not the investigator's work, that raises some of the prickliest questions pertaining to ethics, impartiality, and neutrality. After all, how we ask the question helps determine the answer. Imagine that the employer decides to scope the investigation accordingly.

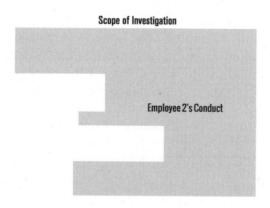

This type of scoping would be entirely appropriate, given the employer's responsibility in paying for the workplace investigation. This approach might succeed in making an investigation more manageable, but it also reveals the degree of power an employer has. Once a complainant brings forward their investigation to the employer, the employer's assumption of liability under relevant laws gives them the authority to determine what is to be investigated. This power is the result of delegating to the employer the enforcement of the duty to investigate. Even where the investigator thinks the other's conduct is worthy of attention, they do not have the power to change the scope. At best, those entire histories turn into an oblique reference or a footnote (e.g., "Employee 1's conduct was not within the scope of this investigation").

These observations speak to an important reality for any respondents who see themselves becoming the focus of workplace investigations. While the obvious admonitions around their conduct in an investigation remain true— cooperate with the investigation, present oneself in a good light, provide any relevant evidence, do not retaliate—thinking about how the scope of the investigation frames questions of responsibility is important. Certainly, a court reviewing a workplace investigation that has been improperly scoped may draw unfavorable inferences. For example, if Employee 2 in the diagram above asserts counter-complaints against Employee 1 that cannot be ignored, it may look scurrilous for an employer to ignore those claims in their scoping decisions. In many cases, the most effective way for a respondent to address an allegation against them is to cross-complain, a phenomenon that also occurs in civil litigation, by drowning the employer and investigator with resource challenges in fully investigating a claim. Moreover, raising concerns about the impartiality of the scope, the investigator, and all kinds of procedural issues can draw into question whether the scope is truly impartial.

But where would it end?

Unsurprisingly, scoping decisions such as these are significant and important sites of power and subtle zones of influence. They can not only impact but also predetermine outcomes, as the party in control of the investigation determines what is investigated. This aspect of control over the process is a design feature of workplace investigations, not a defect. It is one of the most important moments in the process.

It should not be a surprise that maintaining power over the scope would have an impact on the outcome. In 2012, Texas redistricted its 2nd Congressional District, in such a manner that it excluded Beaumont, a city whose population was 46.87 percent Black, even though Beaumont had been part of the 2nd Congressional District for over a century. It was removed along with all of Jefferson County. The new district resembled the type of salamander-shaped districts created by nineteenth-century Governor Elbridge Gerry of Massachusetts, which gave birth to the phrase "gerrymander."[9] The result was a district whose shape undoubtedly impacted, some might say determined, the outcome of the subsequent congressional election:[10]

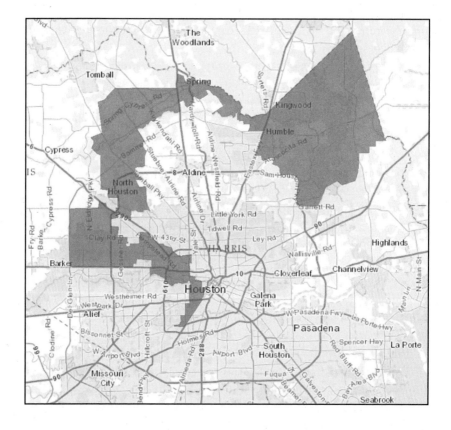

Scoping exhibits the same tendencies as gerrymandering. Although an employer might not directly dictate the outcome of an investigation, their power to scope the investigation may indirectly achieve the same ends. In some cases, these decisions can come dangerously close to violating the well-known idiom of *nemo iudex in causa sua* (no one should be a judge in their own cause). In any case, it is also doubtful that average citizens trust the employer to exercise this decision-making power in a fair manner. Trust in major corporations is about half of what it is in the justice system and courts.[11] Much of that has to do with safeguards. Judges are public appointees and enjoy judicial independence through protected appointments (although this is changing due to workplace investigations of judges themselves).

Procedures are clarified in civil codes. Except in rare cases, courts are open. Moreover, in civil litigation, parties have opportunities to argue over the nature of the allegations themselves. None of the same rules apply in the workplace, which is why the scoping decisions of an employer are even more critical.

Unfortunately, there are few solutions to the problem, short of changing the way liability is assigned. For one thing, it is unwise to give the power of scope to the investigator. The investigator would have a clear conflict of interest. Letting them alter the scope of an investigation, such as permitting it to expand, could be in the investigator's direct financial self-interest, since it would allow them to create more work for themselves to bill the employer-client.

Moreover, investigations that are not properly scoped have the capacity to turn into completely arbitrary fishing expeditions in their own right. We have seen this game before. In 1994, the Clinton administration sought to dispel the Whitewater real estate controversy by appointing a special prosecutor, Robert B. Fiske, to conduct an investigation over which the special prosecutor had full, unhindered scope. Fiske's replacement, Kenneth Starr, continued that investigation for four years. He expanded the scope of the investigation to include various other allegations, including into President Clinton's sexual relationship with former White House intern Monica Lewinsky, an investigation that led to the impeachment of Clinton by the House of Representatives in 1998. That scandal and the impeachment trial were widely seen as a partisan and personal attack on Clinton, rather than a legitimate inquiry into his conduct as president. The Starr investigation was a clear example of how investigations that are not properly scoped can turn into completely arbitrary fishing expeditions in their own right.

We should not pretend that scoping decisions themselves are neutral and do not impact investigations, but we should also dispel the assertion that this problem is the investigator's fault. It is not.

CHAPTER FIVE

PROCEDURE

"We have received a complaint raising concerns about certain conduct that you may have engaged in. We take such complaints seriously and have retained the services of a neutral party to conduct an investigation of the allegations. As part of this process, you will have the opportunity to respond to the allegations against you."

–Email to an employee in an investigation

Once a complainant makes their allegations, it can be a long road to the final determination. What happens before that is a lot of procedure. After a complaint is registered, the investigator reviews relevant documents and then usually interviews the complainant and all relevant witnesses. Then, once the record is fully clear and complete, the respondent is given an opportunity to respond to all of the allegations against them.

Except it is rarely this simple.

One of the biggest problems with workplace investigations is that questions of process often overwhelm the application of uniform standards and common sense. Each investigation has its own twists and turns. From sick or absent individuals to new evidence to accommodations, appeals, and delays, just about anything can stymie the process.

The result is that respect for procedural fairness in workplace investigations often ends up protecting people in many situations where common sense should dictate otherwise. This dynamic happens in other legal contexts, too. Take the case of Jason Redmond. In 2017, Redmond, an officer in the Ontario Provincial Police based outside Kingston, Ontario, sexually assaulted an unconscious woman and filmed the assault on his phone for the perverse reason, he stated, "to show that anybody could rape her."[1] In 2018, Redmond was found guilty of sexual assault, obstructing a police investigation, breaching trust, forging documents, and trafficking drugs.[2] Nevertheless, Redmond appealed, effectively allowing him to keep his pay until a "final" adjudication of the matter. In the meantime, he earned well over $100,000 per year for the following five years, without even working a single day.[3]

Many people already accept the axiom that many lawsuits are determined by resources, not merit. Resource questions can weigh equally heavy on workplace investigations, too. Workplace investigations can drag out for very long periods. For example, parties to an investigation can carefully time absences and sick days, taking a long time to schedule interviews and then canceling at the last minute. Coordinating with a representative to attend the process and requesting opportunities to present evidence to contextualize new material may drag things out. Parties might be on vacation or some type of leave. Not seeking to be accused of procedural unfairness, employers can be in a difficult bind between devoting resources to conducting a fulsome investigation and taking what might feel like a shortcut. If their goal was to do things right with a workplace investigation to gain a fully objective telling of the facts, taking any shortcut of procedure can feel like a betrayal of the goal. It often feels safer to defer to more procedure, not less. And since the process can be so enriching for lawyers and investigators themselves, does one think they are likely to counsel against such measures?

Rules prohibiting retaliation in workplace investigations have made these issues even more challenging for employers to navigate. Most bodies that enforce health, safety, and discrimination and harassment laws underscore a zero tolerance for retaliation against complainants who raise complaints and parties that participate in an investigation. They sternly prohibit taking any actions against an employee for opposing an unlawful, or potentially unlawful, employment practice or participating in an investigation. Even when an investigation finishes, taking such actions against an employee can be seen as retaliatory depending on factors like the temporal proximity to the investigation.

But with investigations that drag out, the rules around retaliation become murky. Applying the test for what constitutes retaliation is rarely easy. This creates an environment in which the leveling of a complaint can be an effective tool for an employee who seeks to avail themselves of protections against retaliation. For example, since investigations can take a long time to complete, the fact that an allegation of *potentially* unlawful conduct exists and needs to be investigated might immediately result in delaying the firing of an incompetent employee who has raised such a complaint; to do so otherwise would risk engaging in retaliation. Even where this fear is not always warranted—the EEOC notes that retaliation-based complaints are far more often to end in findings of "no reasonable cause" than substantiation—the fear can grip workplaces in powerful ways.[4]

Employment lawyers are aware of these dynamics. They reflexively counsel employers not to fire employees who raise complaints. The complaint, they know, can serve as a protective layer around the employee. But what is to stop such realities from becoming incentives to lead employees fearing termination to report on one another as a form of insurance to keep their jobs? While workplace investigations arising from the duty to investigate come from laws intended to foster safe, healthy, and discrimination- and harassment-free workplaces, they are open to bad faith use. With a little creativity, everyone can find ways to identify or overstate instances in which their own health and safety have been threatened or their protected characteristics implicated in an adverse action. For example, in the United States, anyone over the age of forty can avail themselves of the anti-age discrimination protections in the federal Age Discrimination in Employment Act, which prohibit discrimination of anyone over that age. A recent continuing legal education seminar I attended in California noted plainly that every one out of two people may have a disability within the meaning of the state's civil rights legislation protecting against disability discrimination. Such statistics make it possible for large numbers of people to invoke various categories of protection.

The problem with this dynamic is that the workplace investigation no longer becomes the agile instrument it was intended to be. Indeed, many of the problems I am identifying with the device come from the fact that it is becoming more formal, not less. This respect for formality, an employer telling themselves they cannot fire an employee simply because the employee has filed a complaint, activating a concern about retaliation, and needing to steward the investigation through a nuanced process to conclusion, often bars us from applying common sense.

We need less obedience to this kind of stricture. Nowhere is this more evident than in how long and drawn-out some workplace investigations become, which is bad for everyone in the process. Employers who want a speedy resolution often get the opposite. Parties to an investigation who want normalcy in the workplace must often adapt to a new, tense status quo. The complainant or respondent may become discouraged if their case is not being investigated quickly. As anyone thrust into the limelight by a workplace investigation would be able to tell you, one of the greatest challenges in communicating a message to a reluctant public—the complainant's challenge of asserting their complaint against an unbelieving system or the respondent's challenge of asserting their innocence in the face of disbelief—is the adversity of repeating oneself.

Sara Ahmed refers to the "communicative labor" of "making the same complaint to different people in the organization."[5] Some might argue that this weeds out non-meriting complaints. But the fact that meritorious complaints filed by workers still take, on average, 543 days for the EEOC to resolve, when they can take just seconds to file, bodes poorly for the state of justice this device offers. For its part, the Department of Education Office for Civil Rights noted in 2017 that there is "no fixed time frame" at all for Title IX investigations into campus sexual misconduct allegations. Private investigations are not always faster. A private workplace investigation at the university where I teach, which began with anonymous complaints against the university's vice-president of finance and administration, took well over a year.[6] Crunching the numbers of my own practice, I calculated my investigations averaged ninety-seven days (although this average included investigations of all types and sizes, including large investigations that were far more time intensive).[7] The effect of all this is that investigations can blow up in costs or drag on for a long time, often turning into political theatres, often in processes that are not even legally binding for the truth they uncover. If that is the case what is the point of the exercise, apart from enriching the lawyers involved and opening wounds to revisit harms law cannot heal?

Such lengthy processes mirror the endlessness of investigations in other contexts, like environmental impact assessments. It is well documented how environmental impact assessments slow down the construction of vital public goods. It is a depressing sign of change. In 1889, the Eiffel Tower became the tallest building in the world after a construction time of only two years and two months (and no deaths).[8] By contrast, the average environmental impact assessment conducted under the National Environmental Policy Act (NEPA) in the United States, a process that occurs before construction on federally owned lands can even take place, is now 4.5 years, rising nearly 50 percent in just the last two decades.[9] As one commentator notes, this estimate likely *understates* the real amount of time, given that it does not measure the amount of time that goes into preparing the documents that initiate this process. Given that impact statements now average more than 650 pages, these preparatory stages are not meagre.[10]

One of the biggest problems with overly proceduralizing workplace investigations, and turning everything into a workplace investigation, is the tendency towards absolutism. This tendency is already on display with regimes like OSHA, which seeks to attain healthy and safe working places by averting risk, but which, in reality, has exhibited a tendency towards trying to avert *all* risks. Environmental assessments now exhibit the same tendency. Many seem to have forgotten that such goals are unattainable without total knowledge. As Mary Douglas and Aaron Wildavsky wrote in *Risk and Culture*, "[b]ecause no one knows it all, there can be no guarantee that the very dangers people seek to avoid are those that actually will harm them the most."[11] The framing of the health and safety issue, they argue, is better focused on asking what risk is acceptable to most people. Building resilience to the unpredictable consequences that eventuate from risks we take is a wiser approach than attempting to anticipate every harm that can exist.

Figures like Douglas and Wildvasky spent much of their lives seeking to reshape policy discussions around safety from "no harm" to "net benefit," a balance between "the potential for harm and/or safety."[12] Procedures that prohibit or prevent any error, they wrote, are simply "trial without error."[13] Striving for absolute perfection in the procedures of workplace investigations might make investigations perfect—totally unimpeachable when brought before a judge—but they miss the mark of the exercise. Wildavsky viewed the rise of the addiction to this type of procedure-for-procedure's-sake as deeply troubling in its consequences on growth and innovation. "The world of public policy," he wrote, "is in danger of becoming all constants and no variables. How will the costs of change be borne if everyone says 'Not me'? The NIMBY reaction (Not In My Back Yard) of those faced with necessary but inconvenient facilities is a potent example."[14]

In many respects, one of the biggest problems is failing to realize that legalism, and endless recourse to law, such as through persistent and unending duties to investigate, cannot solve all the problems we want them to address. The law is simply the rules to negotiate where we disagree, and to come to, and make, judgments. When it becomes the focus of our activity, and when we stop actually making judgments, inertia results.

Philip K. Howard put it powerfully in the following critique of this kind of legalism:

> Law itself, not the goals to be advanced by law, is now our focus. Indeed, the main lesson of law without judgment is that law's original goal is lost. Safety inspectors wander around without even thinking about safety. The YMCA of New York City, one of the last providers of transient housing at low cost for visitors, gets regular citations for code violations like non-aligning windows and closet doors that do not close tightly. Does the city think that those rooms, by all accounts clean and inexpensive, are somehow unworthy of a city that itself provides cots eighteen inches apart for those who have no place to sleep? A city inspector recently told the YMCA, after it had virtually completed a renovation, that the fire code had changed and a different kind of fire-alarm system, costing another $200,000, would have to be installed. "Don't they realize that the $200,000," said Paula Gavin, the president of New York's YMCA, "can provide year-long programs for a hundred kids?"[15]

Something is amiss. Attempts to safeguard the workplace investigation with more regulation and procedures are unlikely to save it. Emphasizing procedural protections inherently results in complex, time-consuming processes. When this dynamic occurs, responsibility diffuses and delays—dynamics that are already all too common in other contexts. Moreover, few believe that the procedures we have already gone to great lengths to enshrine are even fair. When asked whether they agree with the statement "[c]olleges are fair in the way they treat those *accused* of campus sexual harassment" and whether "[c]olleges are fair in the way they treat those *victims* of campus sexual harassment," a majority of every demographic group by sex, age, and political leaning all disagreed on both accounts.[16] Everyone thinks the processes we have are broken.

Imposing strict procedural requirements seems alluring in this context, but it is likely to exacerbate problems. For example, consider imposing tight time constraints to address the problems of unending investigations. It would, in fact, worsen the process. In 2020, Tennessee proposed a "divisive concepts" bill that would ban teaching sixteen ideas, including the idea that one race or sex is inherently superior or inferior to another race or sex, or that an individual's moral character is determined by the individual's race or sex.[17] Any public institution of higher education receiving a complaint from a student or employee about a breach of this law, according to a procedural requirement embedded in the law itself, would have to investigate that complaint within ten days.[18]

Leaving aside any commentary on the substance of the law itself, consider the consequences. Mandating shorter timelines like these may seem desirable for producing faster outcomes, but doing so may impact fairness and hinder the use of common sense. What if a critical witness is sick during the ten-day period and unable to participate in the investigation? What if the public institution of higher education receives a deluge of frivolous and targeting complaints, each of which it has a duty to investigate under the current law without adequate resources? How does a public institution of higher education balance allocating resources for meritorious complaints in such circumstances? And what about anonymous complaints, where the complainant's refusal to participate challenges the investigator's ability to gather all evidence? The current Tennessee law invites all these hiccups to occur. And yet it permits public institutions of higher education to fire employees after just two complaints are sustained.[19] Overly tight procedural shackles can be a fast-track to producing even more unjust outcomes.

To be sure, timely outcomes matter to justice. But imposing timelines can risk biasing outcomes, and not in the way parties might expect. Fairness plays a crucial role in legitimizing the devices we use to make findings of fact. Parties feeling bereft of procedural fairness will view such processes as illegitimate. Of course, one might not particularly care, especially if the procedure ensures outcomes that one already wants or supports. But normalizing procedures that do so means when the figures in power shift, as they always do, those unscrupulous procedures will be weaponized in the other direction. Respect for the type of precedent needed to stabilize our institutions and strengthen the rule of law often means honoring the rules for those with whom we disagree most. But this is something far too many of us are unwilling to do.

CHAPTER SIX

SECRECY

There is an oft-cited dictum that justice must not only be done, it must also be seen to be done.[1] Unfortunately, workplace investigations are often overly opaque processes, a feature of their proprietary nature. The delegation of responsibility to employers to make workplaces safe, healthy, and free of discrimination and harassment does not make this particularly surprising. After all, if it is the employer's duty to fulfill this obligation, *how* they execute it is up to them.

There are many questions that arise in the shadows of the relationship between the investigator and the client. To preserve the integrity of the workplace as a vehicle of justice, these shadows deserve to be illuminated. For example, questions about scoping decisions should, at a minimum, be included in an investigative report. What was included and excluded, and why? Other questions also deserve to be addressed: How often (and how long) did the investigator meet or communicate with the client? Did they do so during the pendency of the investigation? Are those meetings or communications included in the report, such as in an appendix? Did the final form of the investigation, a short or full report, change because of findings that came up during the investigation? Was the investigator aware of how their report would be used, and did that knowledge impact the product it ultimately turned into? In other words, did the investigator not have any sense of what the client wanted to do with the report and how they planned to use it?

These are hard questions to resolve, but the muddiest questions surround the issue of attorney–client privilege. Communications that an investigator has with parties in an investigation, including parties to the investigation and the employer, form part of the investigative record. When this work is conducted by lawyer-investigators in the context of an attorney–client relationship, the employer can claim privilege, arguing it is not subject to disclosure. However, if the employer decides to disclose the record, waiving the privilege, they can do so. This approach lets employers use workplace investigations as both a sword and a shield. If the employer believes the investigation casts them in a good light, they can offer up the investigation in any formal legal proceeding as a defense of their conduct. If the employer thinks it does not cast them in a good light, they can prevent its disclosure.

This would be a good place to start changing things. Rather than letting employers enjoy unfettered privilege of an investigative file under unexamined ideas of privilege, we should remember that the employer conducts most investigations in the course of business, that is, in response to legal duties to conduct investigations. Like other records created in the course of business, employers should not be able to hide all these records as "legal advice." And yet that is exactly what we are letting them do. The result is a depressing lack of transparency. Parties to investigations are not even always informed about outcomes. An industry-wide survey conducted using case management software for employee relations issues shows that, for Fortune 100 companies, "consistent with the past three years, only 17 percent of organizations share investigation outcomes with employees."[2] This track record does little to inspire faith in the device. Imagine going to court and only finding out what the judge decided 17 percent of the time. What type of faith would people have in the formal justice system?

The shortcomings of this type of secrecy are apparent when we consider a tactic now becoming commonly favored by parties who feel aggrieved by the process, namely, filing lawsuits and other formal review processes. Workplace investigations rarely make legal findings. As a result, their findings are rarely binding on courts. As the Cuomo investigation shows, sometimes the workplace investigation is just a prelude to litigation. But apart from such cases, another reason for filing claims in court is just to obtain the investigative record itself. At my own university, a workplace investigation that involved the investigation of fifty-five complaints against two respondents concluded with none of the complaints against one of the respondents sustained.[3] That investigation cost $1 million, significant money for a university whose total budget is $170 million, and resulted in frequent negative publicity.[4] And yet even at the end of the process, the university did not release the report; it expended more money preparing marketing and executive materials.[5] Parties had to file lawsuits to obtain it. This is what one of the respondents did,[6] alleging the complainants had engaged in "under-handed, secretive, reprehensible, insulting, high-handed, spiteful, malicious and oppressive conduct" by trying "to expose the [subject of the allegations in the investigation] to hatred, ridicule and/or contempt, and/or to lower him in the estimation of right-thinking people generally, and/or to cause him to be shunned or avoided, all of which has occurred."[7] The complainants, now defendants of the lawsuit, responded by creating a GoFundMe to pay for their legal fees.

Better transparency may have avoided these issues. Transparency can respond to the public interest in ways that secrecy never can. As justice moves toward privatization through these devices, we risk paying a price for this lack of transparency (on top of the price we are already paying). Parties who do not know how a system works, makes its decisions, or gives them an opportunity to be heard will come to mistrust its legitimacy and authority. "Everything secret degenerates," Lord Acton once said, "even the administration of justice; noting is safe that does not show how it can bear discussion and publicity." This is one of the reasons why I believe sharing complaints *and* final investigative reports with complainants and respondents—not modified reports or executive summaries of reports but the final report, with redactions as necessary to protect privacy—is so important. It is a sad irony that a device intended to provide closure by making findings of fact is so often unwilling to give that closure to the people it involves.

A system that does not invite opportunities for review and accountability of its decision-making only heightens concerns that those systems will be prepared to take shortcuts. By contrast, some of the healthiest workplace investigations, and those that enjoy the greatest legitimacy in the public eye, are those that are transparent, including where the final report is published and made available. For example, the report that resulted from the investigation pertaining to allegations against the Chicago Police Department concerning its pattern of using force, including deadly force, in violation of the Fourth Amendment of the Constitution, was published in full and strongly recognized as legitimate. In Canada, the investigation done into allegations against Governor General Julie Payette was published online in full, with only minimal personal information redacted. Both processes were broadly endorsed by commentators as legitimate.

Transparency is also necessary to address another important issue: costs. Since certain parties are enriching themselves from these procedures, it makes sense to ask about the price. Yet such information is rarely available to parties and the public. For example, when someone sought the engagement letter for the third-party workplace investigator CBC retained in November 2014 to investigate allegations against Jian Ghomeshi, CBC redacted the hourly rate of the law firm doing the investigation as confidential information.[8] Very little information about the specific costs of these procedures is publicly available. One employment practices liability insurer in California publishes online a list of its approved investigators, showing a flat hourly rate of $290 (current to May 2023) for workplace investigator lawyers.[9] But the billing rate of private firms varies considerably, and total costs are often harder to estimate, given the timeline for investigations can be so unpredictable.

Secrecy also concerns the investigative record itself. Workplace investigations make findings of fact. This is a fraught exercise when the record is not clear and transparent about *how* any findings were made. Unfortunately, in many jurisdictions, in particular in the United States, it is still not required to record interviews. The Association of Workplace Investigators itself equivocates on this issue, stating that workplace investigators should *document* interviews, such as through "[n]ote-taking, recording, or some other method."[10] But an investigator's notes can be very subjective; a recorded interview made available to all removes some of that subjectivity. Unfortunately, it is not the investigator's decision to record or not record an interview. This decision is one of scope and belongs to the employer.

Ultimately, it will be up to legislatures to bolster principles of transparency. Requiring investigators to share information about a complaint or questions with interviewees in advance, and to record interviews and share transcripts or copies of those interviews afterwards, as well as other parts of an investigative file, would dramatically transform the process for participants in many investigations. But until legislatures take such measures, employees will have to fend for themselves in making these requests. And employers will make decisions in ways calculated to serve their advantage. Their calculations often fall on the side of giving the employee as limited information as possible.

Transparency is at the heart of justice because it is essential to knowing the truth. One thing that made the George Floyd murder such a visceral moment for justice was the transparency of the video filmed by seventeen-year-old Darnella Frazier that showed the real story of Floyd's murder and completely rebutted the official narrative from the Minnesota Police Department. The immediate release of the video to the public allowed all of us to be the judge of that crime. It is this type of transparency that is often disappearing in a world of workplace investigations paid for and scoped by employers.

The Cambridge Analytica scandal has a lot to teach us when it comes to transparency of investigations. Although few recall this aspect of the scandal, it gave rise to a massive investigation by Facebook.

In 2007, Facebook launched the Facebook Platform, which allowed third-party software app developers to create apps integrated with the Facebook platform.[11] As the company noted, it sought to increase daily active user count and engagement "by developing products that are more compelling for our users."[12] The Facebook Platform provided to app developers a series of tools and interfaces for them to build apps or to integrate their websites with Facebook,[13] subject to certain policies.[14] Until 2014, Facebook permitted these developers to access not only Facebook user data[15] but also the data for the friends of those users.[16] One of these apps was called "this is your digital life," a personality quiz, which approximately 300,000 people filled out.[17] As the Facebook Platform permitted, its developer, Alexander Kogan, collected not only the Facebook user data of these individuals but also of their friends—87 million users.[18] Facebook learned about Kogan's conduct in December 2015, and requested certification that all Facebook user data be deleted,[19] without taking further action to enforce this request.[20] Instead of doing so, Kogan proceeded to sell the data to Cambridge Analytica, which used it to create targeted political advertisements, including for the successful 2016 presidential campaign of Donald Trump.[21]

These advertisements on Google, Snapchat, X, Facebook, and YouTube featured tailored messages that were used to target 10,000 different ads to different audiences in the months leading up to the 2016 presidential election.[22] They were viewed billions of times.[23]

In March 2018, *The Guardian* and *The New York Times* published simultaneous coverage of the scandal.[24] When the story broke, Facebook announced it would initiate an investigation into "all apps that had access to large amounts of information before [Facebook] changed [its] platform in 2014 to reduce data access" and said it was "conducting a full audit of any app with suspicious activity."[25] The investigation, known as the App-Developer Investigation (ADI), sought to restore trust in the core product. The price of Facebook's stock dropped 7 percent the first day of stock market trading after the story broke,[26] and #deletefacebook began trending.[27] As a result of the barrage of negative publicity, CEO Mark Zuckerberg testified before Congress for the first time.[28] In his testimony, Zuckerberg repeated Facebook was "conducting a full investigation into every single app that had access to a large amount of information before we locked down [the] platform to prevent developers from accessing this information around 2014."[29] Many of these statements about the investigation were publicly available, including on Facebook's own website.[30] In another statement, Facebook revealed it suspended "tens of thousands" of apps in its review of "millions of apps."[31] To plan and execute the ADI with its own internal counsel, Facebook hired Gibson, Dunn & Crucher LLP,[32] tasking it with developing "an investigative framework that reflected counsel's assessment of which types of apps pose the greatest legal risks, how Facebook should prioritize its review of apps in light of these risk assessments, and when Facebook should pursue further action."[33] As part of the investigation, Gibson Dunn hired "as many as 30 internal and external experts,"[34] including non-legal forensic firms.[35]

Facebook never made the investigation public. In March 2018, Massachusetts Attorney General Maura Healey announced on X she was launching her own investigation into Facebook's conduct.[36] Beginning in April 2018, she issued demands for the investigative records.[37] Facebook maintained the information sought from the ADI file "was protected as an attorney work product and by the attorney client privilege."[38] Although Facebook complied with some requests, it refused to comply with several key ones.[39]

This might seem like an arcane dispute, but whether privilege applied to the investigative record is a question that is deeply relevant to workplace investigations. To put it roughly, materials that a business creates in the normal course of business are generally capable of being demanded in a subsequent lawsuit. By contrast, records created by lawyers as part of, or in anticipation of, a lawsuit are not. This is the same argument that underpins barring disclosure of workplace investigation materials when employers do not want to share them.

As any employer might do when faced with a request to see its investigative files, Facebook underscored it was preparing for a lawsuit.[40]

Never mind that most of the work was not done by lawyers, just at their direction, Facebook argued that privilege extended to any documents or materials generated by the ADI because of anticipated litigation,[41] even though it was one of just many investigations set in the course of Facebook's normal enforcement efforts conducted in the regular course of business to "detect, escalate, investigate, and combat violations of Facebook's policies."[42] Ultimately, the appellate court held that the ADI investigation was distinct from ongoing efforts to enforce the company's policies, because of the focus on "past violations, not ongoing operations"[43] and because it served to assist Facebook in its defense of "the vast litigation it is facing."[44] While the court acknowledged Facebook's purpose in conducting the investigation was "to improve the Platform and remedy the loss of user trust,"[45] it noted such a fact did not dismiss the question of whether the materials were prepared in anticipation of litigation.[46] It was an unhelpful judgment for transparency of investigations.

Ultimately, these types of arguments need to be countered by courts or legislatures, by ensuring that investigative records produced as part of an investigation are considered documents prepared in the normal course of business. If we are going to outsource justice to employers, we should insist that the processes be as transparent as possible. Making sure that the secrecy of workplace investigations comes to an end is a necessary first step to accountability.

CHAPTER SEVEN

CONCLUSION

Throughout this short book, I have presented some ideas about how to make workplace investigations a better vehicle for justice. These ideas revolve, in the main, around making workplace investigations, both their procedures and their products, more transparent. If parties in an investigation are looking for any answers in this work, they can be summarized by taking measures to resist the secrecy of workplace investigations.

On that front, some of the ideas I have put forward include the following. As much as possible, the investigative process and the outcome should be transparent. Sunlight truly is the best disinfectant. At the process level, sharing complaints and reports, as well as recording interviews and giving parties transcripts of those interviews and an opportunity to correct wrong information, is a good place to start. Courts and legislatures also need to do far more to reign in the use of attorney–client privilege to shield investigative reports from disclosure. The current state of affairs, which lets employers elect to release a report when it is favorable but not do so when it is not, does not build trust in the device.

Some other obvious transparency measures include making sure the complaint covered by the scope of the investigation reflects the true intent of the complainant, making the complaint available to affected parties (especially the respondent), recording and documenting all aspects of the investigation, and keeping records related to the investigation itself, including meetings, phone calls, and any other communications between the employer and the investigator. Additionally, as wary as I am about costs, I believe they also have a role, as they do in the formal justice system. In Grimsby and Niagara Falls, after they experienced a surge in workplace investigation costs, $200 fees were imposed to file integrity complaints. These are recoverable if the complaint is substantiated.[1]

We must also recognize that recourse to the legal system is not always the best way to resolve conflict. Perhaps nothing has exemplified this truth more in recent years than the #MeToo movement. The unleashing of so much painful experience was an opportunity of powerful collective expression, driving conversations that some 70 percent of Americans felt was holding accountable those who commit sexual harassment or assault at work.[2] The same poll noted that 62 percent of complainants in such matters would be more likely to be believed. Speaking the truth became a force of agency for many people. The collective power of all this expression drove change as a movement, not just a moment, reshaping ethical and moral rules around acceptable conduct, especially in the context of heterosexual interactions and relationships. This did more than the high-profile legal disputes marking the era, which were often a letdown.[3]

Part of the problem, as Robyn Doolittle wrote in *Had It Coming: What's Fair in the Age of #MeToo?*, a study of the movement, was the limit of looking at issues through a legal lens where a moral and ethical one was needed. As she wrote: "The bar for what society is willing to tolerate has been moved. It might not be at the desired level yet, *but it's going in the right direction*. Perhaps the most positive development is that people are talking more openly, and even more importantly, listening to each other. Because the more we hear, the more we learn, the harder it will be to turn away [emphasis added]."[4] It is telling that Doolittle's emphasis on what was gained through the #MeToo movement has not emerged from the legal system; it has come from the ethic of how we address these issues with transparency, openness, and discussion.

Perhaps even more importantly, we need to reckon with the broader sociocultural decision we have taken in recent years to make workplace investigations the sole responsibility of employers. Workplace investigations have given justice a proprietary flavor that is deeply disempowering for many participants in the process. Many of the costs of this trade-off are visible when it comes to transparency shortcomings that employers find all too acceptable. An instrument that should be a vehicle for justice is often an opaque one. Such secrecy only risks fostering and enshrining employers' domination over their employees, undermining not only their individual power in the workplace but also their collective power to band together and make demands vis-à-vis their employer.

While many have written about workplace investigations as displaying problems of neutrality, the real issue, in my view, is that they speak to a broader problem with power imbalances. Tackling these problems is the only way to make the device more attentive to and respectful of the interests of parties involved. Transparency and accountability are the right places to start.

NOTES

Introduction

1   Lindsey Boylan (n.d.), LinkedIn, online: https://www.linkedin.com/in/lindsey-boylan-3477bb3.

2   Lindsey Boylan, @LindseyBoylan, Twitter (Dec. 5, 2020), online: https://twitter.com/LindseyBoylan/status/1335282911331950596.

3   Lindsey Boylan, @LindseyBoylan, Twitter (Dec. 5, 2020), online: https://twitter.com/LindseyBoylan/status/1335286368633823232.

4   Lauren Edmonds et al., "Former Andrew Cuomo aide slams the NY Governor's 'toxic team environment', says his staff are 'deathly afraid of him' and find their working lives 'endlessly dispiriting,'" *Daily Mail* (Dec. 6, 2020), online: https://www.dailymail.co.uk/news/article-9024363/New-York-Gov-Andrew-Cuomos-office-toxic-team-environment-former-aide-claims.html.

5   "New York Primary Election Results: 10th Congressional District," *NYT* (Aug. 17, 2020), online: https://www.nytimes.com/interactive/2020/06/23/us/elections/results-new-york-house-district-10-primary-election.html.

6   A search of news stories on news.google.com and *The New York Times* prior to December 5, 2020, shows virtually no media attention. See also the number of likes on Boylan's tweets at the time. Lindsey Boylan, @LindseyBoylan, Twitter (Nov. 25, 2020), online: https://web.archive.org/web/20201125002526/https://twitter.com/LindseyBoylan.

7   New York City Borough President Primary Election Results, *NYT* (July 20, 2021), online: https://www.nytimes.com/interactive/2021/06/22/us/elections/results-nyc-borough-president-primaries.html.

8   Lindsey Boylan, @LindseyBoylan, Twitter (Nov. 25, 2020), online: https://web.archive.org/web/20201207102322/https://twitter.com/LindseyBoylan. ["ew followers: I'm glad you're here. I am about our beloved New York City's recovery. I'm fighting for our Manhattan to become more equitable, livable and sustainable as we rebuild. I've been fighting for these things my whole life. I hope you'll join us. We need you."]

9   Sophia Ankel, "New York governor Andrew Cuomo will receive an Emmy for showing 'leadership' during his daily COVID-19 press briefings," Insider (Nov. 21, 2022), online: https://www.businessinsider.com/andrew-cuomo-new-york-governor-emmy-award-covid-19-briefings-2020-11.

10 Colin Dwyer, "Andrew Cuomo to Receive International Emmy for 'Masterful' COVID-19 Briefings," NPR (Nov. 21, 2020), online: https://www.npr.org/sections/coronavirus-live-updates/2020/11/21/937445923/andrew-cuomo-to-receive-international-emmy-for-masterful-covid-19-briefings.

11 Bernadette Hogan and Carl Campanile, "Dr. Fauci, Andrew Cuomo, AOC nominated for Time's 'Person of the Year,'" *NY Post* (Nov. 27, 2020), online: https://nypost.com/2020/11/27/fauci-andrew-cuomo-aoc-are-time-person-of-the-year-nominees/.

12 AP, "Andrew Cuomo among contenders for Joe Biden's AG: report," *NY Post* (Dec. 11, 2020), online: https://nypost.com/2020/12/11/andrew-cuomo-among-contenders-for-joe-bidens-ag-report/.

13 Ronan Farrow, "Cuomo's First Accuser Raises New Claims of Harassment and Retaliation," *The New Yorker* (March 18, 2021), online: https://www.newyorker.com/news/news-desk/cuomos-first-accuser-raises-new-claims-of-harassment-and-retaliation.

14 Lindsey Boylan, @LindseyBoylan, Twitter (Dec. 13, 2020), online: https://twitter.com/LindseyBoylan/status/1338125549756182529.

15 Lindsey Boylan, @LindseyBoylan, Twitter (Dec. 9, 2020), online: https://twitter.com/LindseyBoylan/status/1336661572345864192.

16 Lindsey Boylan, @LindseyBoylan, Twitter (Dec. 16, 2020), online: https://web.archive.org/web/20201216102704/https://twitter.com/LindseyBoylan

17 Dana Rubinstein and Jesse McKinley, "Former Aide Accuses Cuomo of Sexual Harassment," *NYT* (Dec. 13, 2020, updated Aug. 3, 2021), online: https://www.nytimes.com/2020/12/13/nyregion/cuomo-sexual-harassment.html?searchResultPosition=77.

18 Dana Rubinstein and Jesse McKinley, "Former Aide Accuses Cuomo of Sexual Harassment," *NYT* (Dec. 13, 2020, updated Aug. 3, 2021), online: https://www.nytimes.com/2020/12/13/nyregion/cuomo-sexual-harassment.html?searchResultPosition=77. For an explanation of the laws, see Proskauer, "Governor Cuomo Signs New York State Budget Anti-Harassment Provisions Into Law" (April 13, 2018), online: https://www.proskauer.com/blog/governor-cuomo-signs-new-york-state-budget-anti-harassment-provisions-into-law..

19 Governor Cuomo Releases Finalized Materials and Guidance on New York's Sexual Harassment Prevention Laws," Governor Andrew Cuomo, New York State (Oct. 1, 2018), online: https://web.archive.org/web/20210306012113/https://www.governor.ny.gov/news/governor-cuomo-releases-finalized-materials-and-guidance-new-yorks-sexual-harassment-prevention and Arielle E. Kobetz, et al., "New York State Issues Final Guidance on Sexual Harassment Policy and Training Requirements In Advance of October 9 Effective Date," Proskauer (Oct. 2, 2018), online: https://www.lawandtheworkplace.com/2018/10/new-york-state-issues-final-guidance-on-sexual-harassment-policy-and-training-requirements-in-advance-of-october-9-effective-date/.

20 Maggie Haberman and Jesse McKinley, "How Cuomo's Team Tried to Tarnish One of His Accusers," *NYT* (March 16, 2021, updated Aug. 10, 2021), online: https://www.nytimes.com/2021/03/16/nyregion/cuomo-lindsey-boylan.html.

21 Maggie Haberman and Jesse McKinley, "How Cuomo's Team Tried to Tarnish One of His Accusers," *NYT* (March 16, 2021, updated Aug. 10, 2021), online: https://www.nytimes.com/2021/03/16/nyregion/cuomo-lindsey-boylan.html.

22 Jodi Kantor and Michael Gold, "Roberta Kaplan, Who Aided Cuomo, Resigns from Time's Up," *NYT* (Aug. 9, 2021), online at: https://www.nytimes.com/2021/08/09/nyregion/roberta-kaplan-times-up-cuomo.html.

23 Sharon Otterman, "Nation's Largest L.G.B.T.Q. Advocacy Group in Turmoil Over Cuomo Ties," *NYT* (Aug. 12, 2021), online at: https://www.nytimes.com/2021/08/12/nyregion/alphonso-david-human-right-campaign-cuomo.html.

24 Ronan Farrow, "Cuomo's First Accuser Raises New Claims of Harassment and Retaliation," *The New Yorker* (March 18, 2021), online: https://www.newyorker.com/news/news-desk/cuomos-first-accuser-raises-new-claims-of-harassment-and-retaliation.

25 Lindsey Boylan, "My story of working with Governor Cuomo," Medium (Feb. 24, 2021), online: https://lindseyboylan4ny.medium.com/my-story-of-working-with-governor-cuomo-e664d4814b4e.

Notes

26 Transcript of Howard Zemsky (July 20, 2021), online: https://ag.ny.gov/sites/
    default/files/2021.07.20_howard_zemsky_cleary_11.29.2021.pdf at 33:14-34-14 and
    53:23-24.

27 Transcript of Andrew Cuomo (July 17, 2021), online: https://ag.ny.gov/sites/default/
    files/2023-01/2021.07.17_gamc_cleary_11.09.2021.pdf at 33:14-34-14 and 53:23-24.
    218:19–222:3.

28 Anne L. Clark, Joon H. Kim, et al, "Report of Investigation into Allegations of
    Sexual Harassment by Governor Andrew M. Cuomo," State of New York Office
    of the Attorney General (Aug. 3, 2021), online: https://ag.ny.gov/sites/default/
    files/2021.08.03_nyag_-_investigative_report.pdf at 7 and 73

29 Anne L. Clark, Joon H. Kim, et al, "Report of Investigation into Allegations of
    Sexual Harassment by Governor Andrew M. Cuomo," State of New York Office of
    the Attorney General (Aug. 3, 2021), online: https://ag.ny.gov/sites/default/files/
    2021.08.03_nyag_-_investigative_report.pdf at 4.

30 Lindsey Boylan, "My story of working with Governor Cuomo," Medium (Feb. 24,
    2021), online: https://lindseyboylan4ny.medium.com/my-story-of-working-with-
    governor-cuomo-e664d4814b4e.

31 Lindsey Boylan, "My story of working with Governor Cuomo," Medium (Feb. 24,
    2021), online: https://lindseyboylan4ny.medium.com/my-story-of-working-with-
    governor-cuomo-e664d4814b4e.

32 Jesse McKinley and Luis Ferré-Sadurní, "Ex-Aide Details Sexual Harassment Claims
    against Gov. Cuomo," NYT (Feb. 24, 2021, updated Aug. 10, 2021), online: https://
    www.nytimes.com/2021/02/24/nyregion/cuomo-lindsey-boylan-harassment.
    html?searchResultPosition=74 and Daniel E. Slotnik, "Former Aide Says Cuomo 'Kissed
    Me on the Lips,'" NYT (Feb. 25, 2021), online: https://www.nytimes.com/2021/02/25/
    nyregion/cuomo-sexual-harassment.html?searchResultPosition=73.

33 Jesse McKinley, "Cuomo Is Accused of Sexual Harassment by a 2nd Former Aide," NYT
    (Feb. 27, 2021, updated Sept. 14, 2021), online: https://www.nytimes.com/2021/02/27/
    nyregion/cuomo-charlotte-bennett-sexual-harassment.html?searchResultPosition=
    72.

34 Matt Flegenheimer and Jesse McKinley, "Cuomo Accused of Unwanted Advance at
    a Wedding: 'Can I Kiss You?,'" NYT (March 1, 2021, updated Nov. 10, 2021), online:
    https://www.nytimes.com/2021/03/01/nyregion/cuomo-harassment-anna-ruch.
    html.

35 Jesse McKinley, "Cuomo Is Accused of Sexual Harassment by a 2nd Former Aide," NYT
    (Feb. 27, 2021, updated Sept. 14, 2021), online: https://www.nytimes.com/2021/02/27/
    nyregion/cuomo-charlotte-bennett-sexual-harassment.html?searchResultPosition=
    72.

36 Matt Flegenheimer and Jesse McKinley, "Cuomo Accused of Unwanted Advance at
    a Wedding: 'Can I Kiss You?,'" NYT (March 1, 2021, updated Nov. 10, 2021), online:
    https://www.nytimes.com/2021/03/01/nyregion/cuomo-harassment-anna-ruch.
    html.

37 Jesse McKinley and Dana Rubinstein, "Under Siege over Sex Harassment Claims,
    Cuomo Offers Apology," NYT (Feb. 28, 2021), online: https://www.nytimes.
    com/2021/02/28/nyregion/cuomo-investigation-sex-harassment.html?searchResult
    Position=71.

38 Senator Liz Krueger, @LizKrueger, Twitter (Feb. 24, 2021), online: https://twitter.com/
    LizKrueger/status/1364681712907780097; Ben Max, @TweetBenMax, Twitter (Feb.
    24, 2021), online: https://twitter.com/TweetBenMax/status/1364730877272588291;
    and Dianne Morales, @Dianne4NYC, Twitter (Feb. 22, 2021), online: https://twitter.
    com/Dianne4NYC/status/1363883882723086338.

39 Archived: US Rep. Kathleen Rice, @RepKathleenRice, Twitter (March 1, 2021), online: https://twitter.com/RepKathleenRice/status/1366558621232939015.

40 Jesse McKinley and Dana Rubinstein, "Under Siege over Sex Harassment Claims, Cuomo Offers Apology," *NYT* (Feb. 28, 2021), online: https://www.nytimes.com/2021/02/28/nyregion/cuomo-investigation-sex-harassment.html.

41 Luis Ferré-Sadurní, "Luis Ferré-Sadurní," *NYT* (March 2, 2021, updated March 16, 2021), online: https://www.nytimes.com/2021/03/02/nyregion/cuomo-sexual-harassment-testify.html?action=click&module=RelatedLinks&pgtype=Article. The specific law was New York Consolidated Laws, Executive Law - EXC § 63(8).

42 Luis Ferré-Sadurní, "Here's How the Cuomo Sexual Harassment Investigation Could Play Out," *NYT* (March 2, 2021, updated March 16, 2021), online: https://www.nytimes.com/2021/03/02/nyregion/cuomo-sexual-harassment-testify.html?action=click&module=RelatedLinks&pgtype=Article and Jesse McKinley and Luis Ferré-Sadurní, "Cuomo Is Told to Preserve Records at Issue in Sexual Harassment Inquiry," *NYT* (online March 5, 2021, updated March 9, 2021), online: https://www.nytimes.com/2021/03/05/nyregion/cuomo-investigation-sexual-harassment.html.

43 Jeff Preval, "You paid for it: Top attorneys making $750 per hour to investigate Governor Cuomo," 2WGRZ (NBC), online: https://www.wgrz.com/article/news/local/you-paid-for-it-top-attorneys-making-750-per-hour-to-investigate-governor-cuomo/71-01dee026-99fb-4f6e-8793-722a3912544f.

44 Jeff Preval, "You paid for it: Top attorneys making $750 per hour to investigate Governor Cuomo," 2WGRZ (NBC), online: https://www.wgrz.com/article/news/local/you-paid-for-it-top-attorneys-making-750-per-hour-to-investigate-governor-cuomo/71-01dee026-99fb-4f6e-8793-722a3912544f.

45 Joshua Solomon, "Taxpayers on Hook," Times Union (Dec. 1, 2021, updated Dec. 2, 2021), online: https://www.timesunion.com/state/article/23-million-in-state-contracts-related-Cuomo-16667118.php.

46 Luis Ferré-Sadurní and Jesse McKinley, "Cuomo Says He Won't Bow to 'Cancel Culture' and Rejects Calls to Resign," *NYT* (online: March 12, 2021, updated March 19, 2021), online: https://www.nytimes.com/2021/03/12/nyregion/cuomo-resign-congress.html?searchResultPosition=326.

47 Daniel E. Slotnik, "Poll Finds Public Support for Cuomo in Spite of Scandals," *NYT* (online March 16, 2021, updated Aug. 10, 2021), online: https://www.nytimes.com/2021/03/16/nyregion/governor-cuomo-polls-sexual-harassment.html?searchResultPosition=308.

48 Luis Ferré-Sadurní and Jesse McKinley, "Cuomo Says He Won't Bow to 'Cancel Culture' and Rejects Calls to Resign," *NYT* (online: March 12, 2021, updated March 19, 2021), online: https://www.nytimes.com/2021/03/12/nyregion/cuomo-resign-congress.html?searchResultPosition=326.

49 Shane Goldmacher, "The Imperious Rise and Accelerating Fall of Andrew Cuomo," *NYT* (March 13, 2021, updated Nov. 10, 2021), online: https://www.nytimes.com/2021/03/13/us/politics/andrew-cuomo-scandals.html?searchResultPosition=319.

50 The Editorial Board, "Can Andrew Cuomo Continue to Lead," *NYT* (March 13, 2021), online: https://www.nytimes.com/2021/03/13/opinion/andrew-cuomo.html?searchResultPosition=318.

51 Daniel E. Slotnik, "Poll Finds Public Support for Cuomo in Spite of Scandals," *NYT* (online March 16, 2021, updated Aug. 10, 2021), online: https://www.nytimes.com/2021/03/16/nyregion/governor-cuomo-polls-sexual-harassment.html?searchResultPosition=308.

Notes

52 Ronan Farrow, "Cuomo's First Accuser Raises New Claims of Harassment and Retaliation," *The New Yorker* (March 18, 2021), online at: https://www.newyorker.com/news/news-desk/cuomos-first-accuser-raises-new-claims-of-harassment-and-retaliation.

53 Luis Ferré-Sadurní, J. David Goodman and William K. Rashbaum, "Cuomo Grilled for 11 Hours in Sexual Harassment Inquiry," *NYT* (Aug. 2, 2021, updated Aug. 10, 2021), online: https://www.nytimes.com/2021/08/02/nyregion/cuomo-sexual-harassment-investigation.html?searchResultPosition=6.

54 Luis Ferré-Sadurní, J. David Goodman and William K. Rashbaum, "Cuomo Grilled for 11 Hours in Sexual Harassment Inquiry," *NYT* (Aug. 2, 2021, updated Aug. 10, 2021), online: https://www.nytimes.com/2021/08/02/nyregion/cuomo-sexual-harassment-investigation.html?searchResultPosition=6 and Luis Ferré-Sadurní and William K. Rashbaum, "After Cuomo's Closest Aides Testify, Now It's His Turn," *NYT* (July 16, 2021, updated Aug. 9, 2021), online: https://www.nytimes.com/2021/07/16/nyregion/andrew-cuomo-investigation.html?searchResultPosition=8.

55 Nicholas Fandos, et al., "Chris Cuomo Played Outsize Role in Ex-Gov. Cuomo's Defense," *NYT* (Nov. 29, 2021, updated Dec. 4, 2021), online: https://www.nytimes.com/2021/11/29/nyregion/chris-cuomo-andrew-cuomo-sexual-harassment.html.

56 "Highly Confidential Video Recorded Testimony of Andrew Cuomo," AG New York (July 17, 2021), online: https://ag.ny.gov/sites/default/files/2023-01/2021.07.17_gamc_cleary_11.09.2021.pdf at 172:14-19.

57 "Andrew Cuomo Sexual Harassment Investigation Transcripts Released," CBS New York (Nov. 10, 2021), online: https://www.cbsnews.com/newyork/news/andrew-cuomo-sexual-harassment-investigation-transcripts-released/.

58 Anne L. Clark, Joon H. Kim, et al, "Report of Investigation into Allegations of Sexual Harassment by Governor Andrew M. Cuomo," State of New York Office of the Attorney General (Aug. 3, 2021), online: https://ag.ny.gov/sites/default/files/2021.08.03_nyag_-_investigative_report.pdf at 15.

59 Anne L. Clark, Joon H. Kim, et al., "Report of Investigation into Allegations of Sexual Harassment by Governor Andrew M. Cuomo," State of New York Office of the Attorney General Letitia James (Aug. 3, 2021), online at: https://ag.ny.gov/sites/default/files/2021.08.03_nyag_-_investigative_report.pdf.

60 Anne L. Clark, Joon H. Kim, et al., "Report of Investigation into Allegations of Sexual Harassment by Governor Andrew M. Cuomo," State of New York Office of the Attorney General Letitia James (Aug. 3, 2021), online at: https://ag.ny.gov/sites/default/files/2021.08.03_nyag_-_investigative_report.pdf at 1-7.

61 Anne L. Clark, Joon H. Kim, et al., "Report of Investigation into Allegations of Sexual Harassment by Governor Andrew M. Cuomo," State of New York Office of the Attorney General Letitia James (Aug. 3, 2021), online at: https://ag.ny.gov/sites/default/files/2021.08.03_nyag_-_investigative_report.pdf at 2.

62 Anne L. Clark, Joon H. Kim, et al., "Report of Investigation into Allegations of Sexual Harassment by Governor Andrew M. Cuomo," State of New York Office of the Attorney General Letitia James (Aug. 3, 2021), online: https://ag.ny.gov/sites/default/files/2021.08.03_nyag_-_investigative_report.pdf at 3.

63 Anne L. Clark, Joon H. Kim, et al., "Report of Investigation into Allegations of Sexual Harassment by Governor Andrew M. Cuomo," State of New York Office of the Attorney General Letitia James (Aug. 3, 2021), online: https://ag.ny.gov/sites/default/files/2021.08.03_nyag_-_investigative_report.pdf at 3.

64 Anne L. Clark, Joon H. Kim, et al., "Report of Investigation into Allegations of Sexual Harassment by Governor Andrew M. Cuomo," State of New York Office of the Attorney General Letitia James (Aug. 3, 2021), online: https://ag.ny.gov/sites/default/files/2021.08.03_nyag_-_investigative_report.pdf at 1.

65 Letitia James, "Independent Investigators Find Governor Cuomo Sexually Harassed Multiple Women, Violated State and Federal Laws," New York State Attorney General (Aug. 3, 2021), online: https://ag.ny.gov/press-release/2021/independent-investigators-find-governor-cuomo-sexually-harassed-multiple-women.

66 Anne L. Clark, Joon H. Kim, et al, "Report of Investigation into Allegations of Sexual Harassment by Governor Andrew M. Cuomo," State of New York Office of the Attorney General (Aug. 3, 2021), online: https://ag.ny.gov/sites/default/files/2021.08.03_nyag_-_investigative_report.pdf.

67 Tierney Speed, "Key findings of the Andrew Cuomo sexual harassment report – and what's next," CNN (Aug. 4, 2021), online: https://www.cnn.com/2021/08/03/politics/cuomo-ag-report-fallout-key-points/index.html.

68 Harmeet Kaur, "These key quotes from Cuomo's resignation speech show he still needs to take more responsibility," CNN (Aug. 10, 2021), online: https://www.cnn.com/2021/08/10/us/cuomo-resignation-speech-quotes-trnd/index.html#:~:text="In%20my%20mind%2C%20I%20have,been%20too%20familiar%20with%20people.

69 Ashley Wong, "Andrew Cuomo Loses His Emmy on Same Day He's Replaced as Governor," NYT (Aug. 24, 2021), online: https://www.nytimes.com/2021/08/24/nyregion/cuomo-emmy.html.

70 Jeffery C. Mays, "Cuomo's Resignation: Shock to Many, Relief to Some, Overdue to Others," NYT (Aug. 10, 2021, updated Aug. 13, 2021), online: https://www.nytimes.com/2021/08/10/nyregion/cuomo-resignation-reaction.html?searchResultPosition=122.

71 Katie Glueck, "As Cuomo Departs, Contenders for Power Begin to Emerge," NYT (Aug. 11, 2021), online: https://www.nytimes.com/2021/08/11/nyregion/governor-democrats-cuomo.html?searchResultPosition=120.

72 Luis Ferré-Sadurní, "Cuomo Continues to Challenge His Accusers as Moving Trucks Are Loaded," NYT (Aug. 20, 2021, updated Nov. 10, 2021), online: https://www.nytimes.com/2021/08/20/nyregion/andrew-cuomo-harassment.html?searchResultPosition=115.

73 Katie Glueck and Dana Rubinstein, "Want to Know Who Might Run for Governor? Check the N.Y. State Fair," NYT (Sept. 1, 2021, updated Oct. 29, 2021), online: https://www.nytimes.com/2021/09/01/nyregion/ny-governor.html?searchResultPosition=113.

74 Katie Glueck and Grace Ashford, "Hochul Locks Up Key Support as Letitia James Begins Statewide Tour," NYT (Oc.t 4, 2021, updated Oct. 27, 2021), online: https://www.nytimes.com/2021/10/04/nyregion/hochul-james-governor.html?searchResultPosition=101.

75 Nicholas Fandos, Katie Glueck and Luis Ferré-Sadurní, "Letitia James Is Preparing Announcement on Run for Governor," NYT (Oct. 27, 2021), online: https://www.nytimes.com/2021/10/27/nyregion/letitia-james-governor-ny.html?searchResultPosition=97.

76 Akash Mehta, "Charges Filed against Andrew Cuomo for Forcible Touching," NY Focus (Oct. 28, 2021), online: https://nysfocus.com/2021/10/28/charges-filed-against-andrew-cuomo-for-criminal-touching/; Luis Ferré-Sadurní, "Groping Charge against Cuomo Is Dismissed," NYT (Jan. 7, 2022), online: https://www.nytimes.com/2022/01/07/nyregion/andrew-cuomo-groping-charge-dismissed.html.

77 Katie Glueck, "Letitia James Declares Her Candidacy for N.Y. Governor," NYT (Oct. 29, 2021, updated Dec. 9, 2021), online: https://www.nytimes.com/2021/10/29/nyregion/letitia-james-governor.html?searchResultPosition=94.

Notes

78 Nicholas Fandos et al., "Chris Cuomo Played Outsize Role in Ex-Gov. Cuomo's Defense," *NYT* (Nov. 29, 2021, updated Dec. 4, 2021), online: https://www.nytimes.com/2021/11/29/nyregion/chris-cuomo-andrew-cuomo-sexual-harassment.html?searchResultPosition=78.

79 Michael Grynbaum, "CNN Fires Chris Cuomo Amid Inquiry into His Efforts to Aid His Brother," CNN (Dec. 4, 2021), online: https://www.nytimes.com/2021/12/04/business/media/chris-cuomo-fired-cnn.html?searchResultPosition=54.

80 Katie Glueck, "Letitia James Drops Out of N.Y. Governor's Race," *NYT* (Dec. 9, 2021), online: https://www.nytimes.com/2021/12/09/nyregion/letitia-james-drops-out-governor.html?searchResultPosition=69.

81 Ed Shanahan, "Prosecutor Won't Charge Cuomo Over Trooper's Sexual Harassment Claim," *NYT* (Dec. 23, 2021), online: https://www.nytimes.com/2021/12/23/nyregion/prosecutor-cuomo-trooper-sexual-harassment-claim.html?searchResultPosition=65; Dana Rubinstein, "Second N.Y. Prosecutor Declines to Seek Criminal Charges against Cuomo," *NYT* (Dec. 28, 2021), online: https://www.nytimes.com/2021/12/28/nyregion/cuomo-prosecution.html?searchResultPosition=64; Luis Ferré-Sadurní and Grace Ashford, "Cuomo Will Not Be Prosecuted in Groping Case, Albany D.A. Says," *NYT* (Jan. 4, 2022), online: https://www.nytimes.com/2022/01/04/nyregion/cuomo-charges.html?searchResultPosition=59 and Grace Ashford, "Last Sex-Crime Inquiry Into Andrew Cuomo Is Dropped," *NYT* (Jan. 31, 2022), online: https://www.nytimes.com/2022/01/31/nyregion/andrew-cuomo-charges.html?searchResultPosition=51.

82 Rebecca Shabad, "Cuomo sued by New York trooper who claimed he sexually harassed her," CNBC (Feb. 18, 2022), online: https://www.cnbc.com/2022/02/18/cuomo-sued-by-new-york-trooper-who-claimed-he-sexually-harassed-her.html and Sonia Moghe and Gregory Krieg, "Accuser sues former New York Gov. Cuomo for sexual harassment and discrimination," CNN (Sept. 15, 2022), online at: https://www.cnn.com/2022/09/14/politics/cuomo-sued-by-accuser/index.html.

83 Zach Williams, "Ex-Gov. Andrew Cuomo demands docs from sexual harassment accuser to fight ongoing lawsuit," *NY Post* (June 6, 2023), online at: https://nypost.com/2023/06/06/ex-gov-andrew-cuomo-demands-docs-from-sexual-harassment-accuser-to-fight-ongoing-lawsuit/.

84 "New York should pay Cuomo's legal fees in suit, judge rules," AP News (Jan. 27, 2023), online at: https://apnews.com/article/new-york-city-andrew-cuomo-lawsuits-8c45dc7449b23ea1e028ed0fbd7f016f.

85 Snejana Farberov, "Andrew Cuomo subpoenas women who accused him of sexual misconduct," *NY Post* (May 4, 2023), online at: https://nypost.com/2023/05/04/andrew-cuomo-subpoenas-accusers-in-sexual-misconduct-case/.

86 Anne McCloy, "Cuomo can use campaign funds to pay legal fees in new lawsuit from former staffer," WNGB Albany (Sept. 14, 2022), online at: https://cbs6albany.com/news/local/gender-discrimination-suit-filed-against-cuomo-three-former-top-aides.

87 Nicholas Fandos and Katie Glueck, "Cuomo Portrays Himself as a Victim in a Six-Figure TV Ad Blitz," *NYT* (Feb. 28, 2022), online: https://www.nytimes.com/2022/02/28/nyregion/andrew-cuomo-tv-ad.html?searchResultPosition=39.

88 Luis Ferré-Sadurní, "Cuomo Re-emerges and Blames 'Cancel Culture' for His Fall," *NYT* (March 6, 2022), online: https://www.nytimes.com/2022/03/06/nyregion/cuomo-cancel-culture-speech.html?searchResultPosition=37.

89 Luis Ferré-Sadurní, "Cuomo Files Ethics Complaint against Letitia James," *NYT* (Sept. 13, 2022), online: https://www.nytimes.com/2022/09/13/nyregion/andrew-cuomo-letitia-james.html?searchResultPosition=2.

90 Luis Ferré-Sadurní, "Cuomo Files Ethics Complaint against Letitia James," *NYT* (Sept.

13, 2022), online: https://www.nytimes.com/2022/09/13/nyregion/andrew-cuomo-letitia-james.html?searchResultPosition=2.

91 James Barron, "Hochul Wins, but It's No Cakewalk," *NYT* (Nov. 9, 2022), online: https://www.nytimes.com/2022/11/09/nyregion/hochul-wins-but-its-no-cakewalk.html?searchResultPosition=8.

92 Jeffery C. Mays, et al., "N.Y. Attorney General's Top Aide Resigns after Sexual Harassment Claims," *NYT* (Dec. 2, 2022), online: https://www.nytimes.com/2022/12/02/nyregion/ibrahim-khan-james-harassment.html.

93 Jeffery C. Mays, et al., "N.Y. Attorney General's Top Aide Resigns after Sexual Harassment Claims," *NYT* (Dec. 2, 2022), online: https://www.nytimes.com/2022/12/02/nyregion/ibrahim-khan-james-harassment.html.

94 Jeffery C. Mays, et al., "N.Y. Attorney General's Top Aide Resigns after Sexual Harassment Claims," *NYT* (Dec. 2, 2022), online: https://www.nytimes.com/2022/12/02/nyregion/ibrahim-khan-james-harassment.html.

95 Jeffery C. Mays, et al., "Letitia James Accused of Protecting Top Aide From Harassment Allegations," *NYT* (Dec. 7, 2022), online: https://www.nytimes.com/2022/12/07/nyregion/letitia-james-victim-khan.html?searchResultPosition=5.

96 Mark Morales, "Republicans call for investigation into NY attorney general's handling of misconduct allegations against chief of staff," CNN (Dec. 6, 2022), online: https://www.cnn.com/2022/12/06/politics/ibrahim-khan-letitia-james/index.html.

97 Ryan King, "Andrew Cuomo announces progressive pro-Israel advocacy group," Washington Examiner (March 14, 2023), online at: https://www.washingtonexaminer.com/policy/foreign/andrew-cuomo-unveils-progressives-israel-group.

Chapter One

1 Donnelly, Matt, "'Ellen DeGeneres Show' Workplace Under Investigation by WarnerMedia," *Variety*, 27 July 2019.

2 Stanton, Sam and Jason Anderson, "'That's who I would hire.' Well-known assault experts leading Walton inquiry for Kings, NBA," *The Sacramento Bee*, 25 April 2019.

3 Villeneuve, Marina, Michael R. Sisak, and Michael Balsamo, "Cuomo to be questioned in sexual harassment investigation," AP, 15 July 2021.

4 Gartenberg, Chaim, "Executives at Google are under investigation by the board for how they handled sexual harassment," *The Verge*, 6 November 2019.

5 Miller, Robyn, "Wabano Centre accused of mishandling funds, workplace harassment," CBC, 29 June 2021.

6 This is the so-called "Tombly/Iqbal" or "Twiqbal" standard. See Bell Atlantic Corp v Twombly, 550 US 544 (2007) and Ashcroft v Iqbal, 556 US 662 (2009).

7 Fed. R. Civ. P. § 8(a)(2).

8 Fed. R. Civ. P. § 8(d)(1).

9 Conklin v. University of British Columbia, 2018 BCHRT 130.

10 Jeffrey Jones, "Confidence in U.S. Institutions Down; Average at New Low," Gallup (July 5, 2022), online at: https://news.gallup.com/poll/394283/confidence-institutions-down-average-new-low.aspx and Pew Research Center, "How to Make Civil Courts More Open, Effective, and Equitable" (Sept. 27, 2023), online at: https://www.pewtrusts.org/en/research-and-analysis/reports/2023/09/how-to-make-civil-courts-more-open-effective-and-equitable.

11 A quick disclaimer about this book. This book does not offer advice. It is not an intensive manual on conducting workplace investigations. Those looking for training on workplace investigations can attend one, such as the standard training offered by

the Association of Workplace Investigators. The book is also not a tell-all of my own investigations. Duties of attorney–client confidentiality and respect for other ethical obligations prohibit me from discussing my investigations, and so the stories I tell here are not mine. They are taken from the public record.

Chapter Two

1 Ashley Burke and Kristen Everson, "Gov. Gen. Payette has created a toxic climate of harassment and verbal abuse at Rideau Hall, sources allege," CBC (July 21, 2020), online: https://www.cbc.ca/news/politics/julie-payette-governor-general-harassment-allegations-1.5657397.

2 Ashley Burke, "Trudeau government refuses to support Gov. Gen. Julie Payette while under scrutiny," CBC (Aug. 7, 2020), online: https://www.cbc.ca/news/politics/deputy-prime-minister-governor-general-claims-1.5678168.

3 Catharine Tunny and Ashley Burke, "Second-in-command at Rideau Hall promises to improve work environment following GG harassment allegations," CBC (July 22, 2020), online: https://www.cbc.ca/news/politics/rideau-hall-harassment-memo-1.5658636.

4 "About Quintet," Quintet Consulting Corporation (n.d.), online: https://quintet.ca.

5 "Ottawa firm hired to review workplace complaints at Rideau Hall," CP (Sept. 1, 2020), online: https://toronto.citynews.ca/2020/09/01/ottawa-firm-hired-to-review-workplace-complaints-at-rideau-hall/.

6 Quintet Consulting was mandated on August 31, 2020, following receipt of the anonymous complaints to address the concerns. See Quintet Consulting Corporation, "Final Review Report," January 12, 2021, at 12 and 15. Retrieved online on April 20, 2021, at <https://www.theglobeandmail.com/files/editorial/News/GG/Report-into-workplace-conditions-at-Rideau-Hall.pdf>.

7 Quintet Consulting was mandated on August 31, 2020, following receipt of the anonymous complaints to address the concerns. See Quintet Consulting Corporation, "Final Review Report," January 12, 2021, at 1. Retrieved online on April 20, 2021, at <https://www.theglobeandmail.com/files/editorial/News/GG/Report-into-workplace-conditions-at-Rideau-Hall.pdf>.

8 Quintet Consulting was mandated on August 31, 2020, following receipt of the anonymous complaints to address the concerns. See Quintet Consulting Corporation, "Final Review Report," January 12, 2021, at 1. Retrieved online on April 20, 2021, at <https://www.theglobeandmail.com/files/editorial/News/GG/Report-into-workplace-conditions-at-Rideau-Hall.pdf>.

9 Quintet Consulting was mandated on August 31, 2020, following receipt of the anonymous complaints to address the concerns. See Quintet Consulting Corporation, "Final Review Report," January 12, 2021, at 54. Retrieved online on April 20, 2021, at <https://www.theglobeandmail.com/files/editorial/News/GG/Report-into-workplace-conditions-at-Rideau-Hall.pdf>.

10 Quintet Consulting was mandated on August 31, 2020, following receipt of the anonymous complaints to address the concerns. See Quintet Consulting Corporation, "Final Review Report," January 12, 2021, at 53–54. Retrieved online on April 20, 2021, at <https://www.theglobeandmail.com/files/editorial/News/GG/Report-into-workplace-conditions-at-Rideau-Hall.pdf>.

11 See Jackson, Hannah, "Report into Julie Payette's conduct says staff reported 'toxic', 'poisoned' work atmosphere," Global News, January 27, 2021. Retrieved online on April 20, 2021, at <https://www.theglobeandmail.com/files/editorial/News/GG/Report-into-workplace-conditions-at-Rideau-Hall.pdf>.

12 Connolly, Amanda, "Gov. Gen. Julie Payette resigning amid 'scathing' Rideau Hall workplace review," *Global News*, Jan. 21, 2021. Retrieved online on April 20, 2021, at <https://globalnews.ca/news/7590462/julie-payette-rideau-hall-toxic-workplace-probe/>.

13 "Read Governor-General Julie Payette's full resignation statement," *The Globe and Mail*, Jan. 21, 2021. Retrieved online on April 20, 2021, at <https://www.theglobeandmail.com/canada/article-statement-from-the-governor-general-julie-payette/>.

14 "Legacy of Hate," CBC (n.d.), online: https://www.cbc.ca/history/EPISCONTENTS E1EP11CH3PA3LE.html.

15 "Achievements in Public Health, 1900–1999: Improvements in Workplace Safety—United States, 1900–1999," CDC (June 11, 1999) 48:22, online: https://www.cdc.gov/mmwr/preview/mmwrhtml/mm4822a1.htm.

16 Donald M. Fisk, "American Labor in the 20th Century," US Bureau of Labor Statistics (Jan. 30, 2003), online: https://www.bls.gov/opub/mlr/cwc/american-labor-in-the-20th-century.pdf.

17 "National Census of Fatal Occupational Injuries in 2021," Bureau of Labor Statistics, US Dept. of Labor (Dec. 16, 2022), online: https://www.bls.gov/news.release/pdf/cfoi. pdf.

18 "Number of coal mining fatalities in the United States from 1900 to 2021," Statista (Nov. 22, 2022), online: https://www.statista.com/statistics/949324/number-occupational-coal-industry-fatalities-united-states/#:~:text=In%202021%20there%20 were%20 ten, in%20the%20US%20that%20year.

19 "Commonly Used Statistics," Occupational Safety and Health Administration (n.d.), online: https://www.osha.gov/data/commonstats.

20 "Work Safety Introduction," National Safety Council (n.d.), online: https://injuryfacts.nsc.org/work/work-overview/work-safety-introduction/.

21 National Safety Council, Accident Facts (1998) Itasca, Illinois: 1998.

22 Steven Pinker, Enlightenment Now: The Case for Reason, Science, Humanism, and Progress, Viking (2018). Find cite.

23 Occupational Safety and Health Act of 1970, ss. 2(b)(12) and 8(c)(1). Further regulations were outlined in 29 CFR Part 1904.

24 OSH Act of 1970; see www.govinfo.gov/content/pkg/STATUTE-84/pdf/STATUTE-84-Pg1590.pdf#page=1.

25 29 USC § 654(a)(1).

26 "Incident Investigation," Occupational Safety and Health Administration (n.d.), online: https://www.osha.gov/incident-investigation#:~:text=OSHA%20strongly%20 encourages%20employers%20to,circumstances%20had%20been%20slightly%20 different.

27 Gillian Shearer, The Law and Practice of Workplace Investigations, Emond (2017) at 13 and 15.

28 Merran Proctor, "Occupational Health and Safety Legislation," The Encyclopedia of Saskatchewan (n.d.), online: https://esask.uregina.ca/entry/occupational_health_ and_safety_legislation.jsp.

29 Health and Safety at Work etc. Act 1974, c 37.

30 Whirlpool Corp. v. Marshall, 445 US 1 (1980).

31 N.A. Stout et al., "Occupational injury mortality rates in the United States: changes from 1980 to 1989," *Am J Public Health* (1996) 86:1, online: https://pubmed.ncbi.nlm.nih.gov/8561247/.

32 "National Census of Fatal Occupational Injuries in 2021," Bureau of Labor Statistics, US Dept. of Labor (Dec. 16, 2022), online: https://www.bls.gov/news.release/pdf/cfoi. pdf.

33 "National Census of Fatal Occupational Injuries in 2021," Bureau of Labor Statistics, US Dept. of Labor (Dec. 16, 2022), online: https://www.bls.gov/news.release/pdf/cfoi.pdf.

34 Ivan Pereira, "Workplaces are the most common mass shooting sites, data shows," ABC (April 11, 2023), online: https://abcnews.go.com/US/workplaces-common-mass-shooting-site-data-shows/story?id=98502802.

35 "America's essential workers are under-protected in the face of covid-19," *The Economist* (May 14, 2020), online: https://www.economist.com/graphic-detail/2020/05/13/americas-essential-workers-are-under-protected-in-the-face-of-covid-19.

36 AFL-CIO, Death on the Job: The Toll of Neglect (April 2019, 28th ed.), online: https://aflcio.org/sites/default/files/2019-05/DOTJ2019Fnb_1.pdf.

37 29 CFR § 1904.1.

38 "US Department of Labor announces annual adjustments to OSHA civil penalties for 2023," Occupational Safety and Health Administration (Jan. 12, 2023), online: https://www.osha.gov/news/newsreleases/trade/01122023#:~:text=Therefore%2C%20new%20OSHA%20penalty%20amounts,violation%20to%20%2415%2C625%20per%20violation.

39 Phillip K. Howard, Death of Common Sense: How Law Is Suffocating America, Grand Central Publish (1996).

40 Phillip K. Howard, Death of Common Sense: How Law Is Suffocating America, Grand Central Publish (1996).

41 42 US Code § 2000e-2.

42 29 CFR § 1604.11. [Noting that "[h]harassment on the basis of sex is a violation of section 703 of title VII."]

43 It applies to employers with more than 15 employees. See 42 US Code § 2000e(b).

44 William M. Welch, "Thomas Presided Over Shift in Policy at EEOC, Records Show," AP (July 25, 1991), online: https://apnews.com/article/b419883e871b5117649d1f3fdacf6f95.

45 "You'll be hearing from my lawyer," *The Economist* (June 19, 1997), online: https://www.economist.com/business/1997/06/19/youll-be-hearing-from-my-lawyer.

46 KC Johnson and Stuart Taylor, "The path to Obama's 'Dear Colleague' letter," *The Washington Post* (Jan. 31, 2017), online: https://www.washingtonpost.com/news/volokh-conspiracy/wp/2017/01/31/the-path-to-obamas-dear-colleague-letter/.

47 Michael Cianfichi and Olabisi Okubadejo, "OCR Withdraws Obama-Era Title IX Guidance," Ballard Spahr LLP (Sept. 27, 2017), online: https://www.jdsupra.com/legalnews/ocr-withdraws-obama-era-title-ix-79616/.

48 R. Shep Melnick, "Analyzing the Department of Education's final Title IX rules on sexual misconduct," Brookings (June 11, 2020), online: https://www.brookings.edu/research/analyzing-the-department-of-educations-final-title-ix-rules-on-sexual-misconduct/.

49 "Handling Internal Discrimination Complaints About Disciplinary Action," EEOC (n.d.), online: https://www.eeoc.gov/employers/small-business/handling-internal-discrimination-complaints-about-disciplinary-action.

50 "Policy Guidance on Current Issues of Sexual Harassment," EEOC (March 19, 1990), online: https://www.eeoc.gov/laws/guidance/policy-guidance-current-issues-sexual-harassment.

51 "Dear Colleague," US Dept. of Education (April 4, 2011), online: https://www2.ed.gov/about/offices/list/ocr/letters/colleague-201104.pdf.

52 Google, "Books Ngram Viewer" (accessed online June 29, 2023), online at: https://books.google.com/ngrams/graph?content=workplace+investigation&year_start=1800&year_end=2019&corpus=en-2019&smoothing=3.

53 Fuller v. City of Oakland, Cal., 47 F.3d 1522, 1525 (9th Cir., 1995).

54 Fuller v. City of Oakland, Cal., 47 F.3d 1522, 1526 (9th Cir., 1995).

55 Valdez v. Church's Fried Chicken, 683 F. Supp. 596, 628 (W.D. Tex 1988).

56 Valdez v. Church's Fried Chicken, 683 F. Supp. 596, 628 (W.D. Tex. 1988).

57 Valdez v. Church's Fried Chicken, 683 F. Supp. 596, 627 (W.D. Tex. 1988).

58 Faragher v. City of Boca Raton, 524 US 775 (1998).

59 Faragher v. City of Boca Raton, 524 US 775 at 778 (1998).

60 Burlington Industries, Inc v. Ellerth, 524 US 742 (1998).

61 Burlington Industries, Inc v. Ellerth, 524 US 742 (1998).

62 Kyle Morris, "Cuomo accuser files lawsuit against New York state, alleging responsibility for sexual harassment," Fox News (March 16, 2023), online at: https://www.foxnews.com/politics/cuomo-accuser-files-lawsuit-against-new-york-state-alleging-responsibility-sexual-harassment.

63 Cotran v. Rollins Hudig Hall International, Inc., 17 Cal 4th 93 - Cal: Supreme Court 1998 at 97

64 Cotran v. Rollins Hudig Hall International, Inc., 17 Cal 4th 93 - Cal: Supreme Court 1998 at 98.

65 Cotran v. Rollins Hudig Hall International, Inc., 17 Cal 4th 93 - Cal: Supreme Court 1998 at 107.

66 42 USC section 2000e-2(a)(1).

67 Eugene Volokh, "Freedom of Speech and Workplace Harassment," UCLA L Review (1991–92) 39 at 1812

68 Björn Lindahl, "Workplace battlegrounds: Are Norwegian employees being criminalised?" Nordic Labour Journal (May 28, 2021), online at: http://nordiclabourjournal.org/nyheter/news-2021/article.2021-05-27.4799329368.

69 Eugene Volokh, "Freedom of Speech and Workplace Harassment," UCLA L Review (1991–92) 39 at 1812.

70 Burlington Industries, Inc. v. Ellerth, 524 US 742 (1998) and Faragher v. City of Boca Raton, 524 US 775 (1998).

71 Dan Schawbel, "Why work friendships are critical for long-term happiness," CNBC (Nov. 13, 2018), online: https://www.cnbc.com/2018/11/13/why-work-friendships-are-critical-for-long-term-happiness.html.

72 "Romance in the Workplace: It's happening, but is it allowed?", ADP (June 25, 2019), online: https://www.adp.ca/-/media/adpca/redesign2019/pdf/adp_q4_19_workplace_relationship_study_press_release_final_for_distribution.pdf?la=en&hash=24C6E3BE65D317D24C6F8A6A5972F07C4D9948B1.

73 Abby Gardner, "Barack and Michelle Obama: A Complete Relationship Timeline," Glamour (Nov. 12, 2020), online: https://www.glamour.com/story/barack-and-michelle-obama-a-complete-relationship-timeline.

74 Alice Munro, "The Bear Came Over the Mountain," The New Yorker (Oct. 14, 2013), online: https://www.newyorker.com/magazine/2013/10/21/the-bear-came-over-the-mountain-2.

75 Doug Saunders, "Marriage may have saved my life, but can it fix the world?" The Globe and Mail (July 1, 2023), online at: https://www.theglobeandmail.com/opinion/article-marriage-may-have-saved-my-life-but-can-it-fix-the-world/.

76 Elizabeth Renzetti, "An elegy for the office romance," The Globe and Mail (Feb. 12, 2022), online at: https://www.theglobeandmail.com/opinion/article-labour-of-love-an-elegy-for-the-office-romance/.

77 Alexandra Olson and Dee-Ann Durbin, "Consent may not be 'truly possible' in some office romances: experts," Global News (Nov. 5, 2019), online: https://globalnews.ca/news/6128365/mcdonalds-ceo-work-relationship/.

78 David Yaffe-Bellany, "McDonald's Fires C.E.O. Steve Easterbrook after Relationship with Employee," *NYT* (Nov. 3, 2019), online: https://www.nytimes.com/2019/11/03/business/mcdonalds-ceo-fired-steve-easterbrook.html.

79 Mae Anderson, "CNN exec Zucker's ouster shows peril of hiding work romance," AP (Feb. 6, 2022), online: https://apnews.com/article/business-lifestyle-arts-and-entertainment-relationships-chris-cuomo-0e13f4272b59cc55169a21f1772b4baa and Tatiana Siegel, "CNN Probe Eyes Jeff Zucker's Ties to Andrew Cuomo," Rolling Stone (Feb. 3, 2022), online at: https://www.rollingstone.com/culture/culture-news/jeff-zucker-cnn-investigation-affair-cuomo-1294608/.

80 "Clients Pay Their Highest Rates to These Law Firms–and They Are Worth It," BTI Consulting Group (June 13, 2018), online at: https://bticonsulting.com/themadclientist/the-highest-rate-firms-2018.

81 Claire Cain Miller, "It's Not Just Mike Pence. Americans Are Wary of Being Alone with the Opposite Sex", *NYT* (July 1, 2017), online: https://www.nytimes.com/2017/07/01/upshot/members-of-the-opposite-sex-at-work-gender-study.html.

82 "Over-friendly, or sexual harassment? It depends partly on whom you ask," *The Economist* (Nov. 17, 2017), online: https://www.economist.com/graphic-detail/2017/11/17/over-friendly-or-sexual-harassment-it-depends-partly-on-whom-you-ask.

83 Eva Illouz, The End of Love: A Sociology of Negative Relations, OUP (2019) at 174.

84 Eva Illouz, The End of Love: A Sociology of Negative Relations, OUP (2019) at 173.

85 "Top 100: The Most Visited Websites in the US," Semrush Blog (March 2023), online: https://www.semrush.com/blog/most-visited-websites/.

86 "All Time Most Viewed Porn Videos in the USA," Pornhub (n.d.), online: https://www.pornhub.com/video?o=mv&t=a&cc=us.

87 Nicole Gallucci, "Just a Jim looking for his Pam: The fictional couples dominating dating app bios" (Feb. 10, 2020), online at: https://mashable.com/article/jim-looking-for-pam-fictional-couple-dating-app-bios.

88 Ill Eva Illouz, The End of Love: A Sociology of Negative Relations, OUP (2019) at 177.

89 For example, California requires that external investigators be state-licensed (or be attorneys). See Cal. Bus. & Prof. Code sections 7520–7539.

90 EEOC, "Enforcement Guidance: Vicarious Liability for Unlawful Harassment by Supervisors." Retrieved online on May 17, 2021, at <https://www.eeoc.gov/laws/guidance/enforcement-guidance-vicarious-liability-unlawful-harassment-supervisors>.

91 For example, the California Department of Fair Employment and Housing provides that an investigator "should be knowledgeable about standard investigatory practices. This includes knowledge of laws and policies relating to harassment, investigating technique relating to questioning witnesses, document interview and analyzing information." See Cal. Dept. Fair Emp. & Hous., "Harassment Prevention Guide for California Employees." Retrieved online May 17, 2021, at <https://www.dfeh.ca.gov/wp-content/uploads/sites/32/2017/06/DFEH-Workplace-Harassment-Guide-1.pdf>.

92 Cal. Bus. & Prof. Code Section 7520. (Requiring that third-party investigators be licensed or attorneys acting in their capacities as attorneys).

93 Andrew H. Friedman and Courtney Abrams, "Attorney Workplace Investigations: Neither Impartial Nor Independent," California Labor and Employer Law Review (Sept. 2022).

94 Jamal Greene, How Rights Went Wrong: Why Our Obsession with Rights Is Tearing America Apart, Mariner Books (2021) at 167.

95 Jamal Greene, How Rights Went Wrong: Why Our Obsession with Rights Is Tearing America Apart, Mariner Books (2021).

96 Kevin Draper, "A Disparaging Video Prompts Explosive Fallout within ESPN," *The New York Times* (July 4, 2021), online at: https://www.nytimes.com/2021/07/04/sports/basketball/espn-rachel-nichols-maria-taylor.html.

97 Steven Phillips Horst and Eric Schwartau, "Talk Hole: Out of Office," Gawker (Aug. 2, 2022), online: https://www.gawker.com/culture/talk-hole-out-of-office.

98 Russell Jacoby, "The Takeover," Tablet (Dec. 18, 2022), online: https://www.tabletmag.com/sections/arts-letters/articles/takeover-russell-jacoby.

99 Lynne Curry, "Emoji harassment is on the rise. Here's how managers and employees can handle it." Anchorage Daily News (March 28,2022), online at: https://www.adn.com/business-economy/2022/03/28/emoji-harassment-is-on-the-rise-heres-how-managers-and-employees-can-handle-it/.

100 Eric Scwartau and Steven Phillips-Horst, "Talk Hole: Welcome to Gawk Hole," Gawker (January 26, 2022), online at: https://www.gawker.com/culture/talk-hole-welcome-to-gawk-hole.

Chapter Three

1 US Equal Employment Opportunity Commission, "Select Task Force on the Study of Harassment in the Workplace" (June 2016), online at: <https://www.eeoc.gov/select-task-force-study-harassment-workplace> (citing Cortina, Lilia M. and Jennifer L. Berdahl, "Sexual Harassment in Organizations: A Decade of Research in Review," The Sage Handbook of Organizational Behavior 469, 469-96 (J. Barling & C. L. Cooper eds., 2008).)

2 Sarah Schulman, Conflict Is Not Abuse: Overstating Harm, Community Responsibility, and the Duty of Repair, Arsenal Pulp Press (2016).

3 Sarah Schulman, Conflict Is Not Abuse: Overstating Harm, Community Responsibility, and the Duty of Repair, Arsenal Pulp Press (2016).

4 Sarah Schulman, Conflict Is Not Abuse: Overstating Harm, Community Responsibility, and the Duty of Repair, Arsenal Pulp Press (2016).

5 Sarah Schulman, Conflict Is Not Abuse: Overstating Harm, Community Responsibility, and the Duty of Repair, Arsenal Pulp Press (2016).

6 Sarah Schulman, Conflict Is Not Abuse: Overstating Harm, Community Responsibility, and the Duty of Repair, Arsenal Pulp Press (2016). Cite.

7 Donald T. Tomaskovic-Devey, "63% of workers who file an EEOC discrimination complaint lose their jobs," The Conversation (July 13, 2021), online at: https://theconversation.com/63-of-workers-who-file-an-eeoc-discrimination-complaint-lose-their-jobs-163048.

8 Denis Campbell, "Almost one in three doctors investigated by GMC 'have suicidal thoughts'," The Guardian (April 27, 2023), online at: https://www.theguardian.com/society/2023/apr/27/almost-one-in-three-doctors-investigated-by-gmc-have-suicidal-thoughts#:~:text=Almost%20one%20in%20three%20UK,Protection%20Society%20(MPS)%20said.

9 Jian Ghomeshi, "Reflections from a Hashtag," New York Review of Books (Oct. 11, 2018), online at: https://www.nybooks.com/articles/2018/10/11/reflections-hashtag/.

10 Ian Buruma, "Doing the Work," Harper's Magazine (2023), online at: https://harpers.org/archive/2023/07/protestant-ethic-and-the-spirit-of-wokeness/.

11 Ian Buruma, "Doing the Work," Harper's Magazine (2023), online at: https://harpers.org/archive/2023/07/protestant-ethic-and-the-spirit-of-wokeness/.

12 Ian Buruma, "Doing the Work," Harper's Magazine (2023), online at: https://harpers.org/archive/2023/07/protestant-ethic-and-the-spirit-of-wokeness/.

Notes

13 Sarah Schulman, Conflict Is Not Abuse: Overstating Harm, Community Responsibility, and the Duty of Repair, Arsenal Pulp Press (2016). *Cite.*

14 Ahmad, Sara, Complaint!, Duke University Press (2021) at 44.

15 Phillip K. Howard, Death of Common Sense: How Law Is Suffocating America, Grand Central Publish (1996) at 21.

16 Maya Binyam, "You Pose a Problem: A Conversation with Sara Ahmed," The Paris Review (2022), online: https://www.theparisreview.org/blog/2022/01/14/you-pose-a-problem-a-conversation-with-sara-ahmed/.

17 Ahmad, Sara, Complaint!, Duke University Press (2021) at 44.

18 Ahmad, Sara, Complaint!, Duke University Press (2021) at 25.

19 "Protected Identity Harm Reporting," Stanford University (n.d.), online: https://protectedidentityharm.stanford.edu.

20 Jason Fekete et al., "Trudeau suspends two Liberal MPs from caucus for alleged 'personal misconduct,'" Ottawa Citizen (Nov. 6, 2014), online: https://ottawacitizen.com/news/politics/two-liberal-mps-investigated-for-personal-misconduct#:~:text=Trudeau%20the%20faced%20journalists%20to,another%20party%2C"%20sad%20Trudeau.

21 Janet DiGiacomo, "Woman who accused Justin Trudeau of groping breaks her silence," CNN (July 6, 2018), online: https://edition.cnn.com/2018/07/06/americas/justin-trudeau-groping-allegations/index.html.

22 Daniel Dale, "Donald Trump fires Anthony Scaramucci over his vulgar remarks, unpredictability," Toronto Star (Jan. 9, 2017), online: https://www.thestar.com/news/world/2017/07/31/anthony-scaramucci-out-as-white-house-communications-director-after-10-days-on-the-job.html.

23 Rupa Jose et al., "Political Differences in American Reports of Sexual Harassment and Assault," *Journal of Interpersonal Violence* (2019) 36:15–16, online: https://journals.sagepub.com/doi/abs/10.1177/0886260519835003?journalCode=jiva.

24 Monica Anderson, "Democrats more likely than Republicans to say online harassment is a major problem," Pew Research Center (July 24, 2017), online: https://www.pewresearch.org/short-reads/2017/07/24/democrats-more-likely-than-republicans-to-say-online-harassment-is-a-major-problem/.

25 Alexa Lardieri, "Poll: Democrats and Republicans Split on Sexual Harassment," US News (April 4, 2018), online: https://www.usnews.com/news/politics/articles/2018-04-04/poll-democrats-and-republicans-split-on-sexual-harassment.

26 Alexa Lardieri, "Poll: Democrats and Republicans Split on Sexual Harassment," US News (April 4, 2018), online: https://www.usnews.com/news/politics/articles/2018-04-04/poll-democrats-and-republicans-split-on-sexual-harassment. See also Costa Panagopoulos et al., "Liberals and conservatives see sexual harassment complaints very differently. This explains why," Washington Post (Dec. 14, 2018), online: https://www.washingtonpost.com/news/monkey-cage/wp/2018/12/14/liberals-and-conservatives-see-sexual-harassment-claims-very-differently-this-explains-why/.

27 Ipsos, "Ipsos/NPR Examine Views on Sexual Harassment and Assault" (Oct. 31, 2018), online; https://www.ipsos.com/en-us/news-polls/NPR-Sexual-Harassment-and-Assault.

28 Rupa Jose et al., "Political Differences in American Reports of Sexual Harassment and Assault," Journal of Interpersonal Violence (2019) 36:15–16, online: https://journals.sagepub.com/doi/abs/10.1177/0886260519835003?journalCode=jiva at 7714.

29 Rupa Jose et al., "Political Differences in American Reports of Sexual Harassment and Assault," *Journal of Interpersonal Violence* (2019) 36:15–16, online: https://journals.sagepub.com/doi/abs/10.1177/0886260519835003?journalCode=jiva at 7714.

30 Emily Ekins, "Poll: 62% of Americans Say They Have Political Views They're Afraid to Share," Cato Institute (July 22, 2020), online: https://www.cato.org/survey-reports/poll-62-americans-say-they-have-political-views-theyre-afraid-share#liberals-are-divided-political-expression.

31 Katie Reilly, "Republicans are Increasingly Targeting 'Divisive Concepts' at Colleges and Universities," *Time* (March 29, 2022), online: https://time.com/6162489/divisive-concepts-colleges/#:~:text=As%20of% March%2028%2C%20 at,at%20stay%20 with%20such%20 laws.

32 Claire M. Gothreau et al., "Looking the other way: how ideology influences perceptions of sexual harassment," *European Journal of Politics and Gender* (2022) 5:2, online: https://bristoluniversitypressdigital.com/view/journals/ejpg/5/2/article-p211.xml.

33 Claire M. Gothreau et al., "Looking the other way: how ideology influences perceptions of sexual harassment," *European Journal of Politics and Gender* (2022) 5:2, online: https://bristoluniversitypressdigital.com/view/journals/ejpg/5/2/article-p211.xml.

34 Ipsos, "Ipsos/NPR Examine Views on Sexual Harassment and Assault" (Oct. 31, 2018), online: https://www.ipsos.com/en-us/news-polls/NPR-Sexual-Harassment-and-Assault.

35 Jason Armesto, "Politics increasingly a deal-breaker on US dating scene," BBC (Oct. 26, 2022), online: https://www.bbc.com/news/world-us-canada-63180007.

36 Jamal Greene, How Rights Went Wrong: Why Our Obsession with Rights Is Tearing America Apart, Mariner Books (2021) at xxviii.

37 42 USC. § 2000e-8(c) and 29 CFR 1602.7-.14 and 41 CFR 60-1.7(a).

38 See, e.g., Harvard University, Self-Identification at Harvard, online: https://edib.harvard.edu/self-id-harvard.

39 Philip Mousavizadeh, "A 'proliferation of administrators': faculty reflect on two decades of rapid expansion," *Yale News* (November 10, 2021), online at: https://yaledailynews.com/blog/2021/11/10/reluctance-on-the-part-of-its-leadership-to-lead-yales-administration-increases-by-nearly-50-percent/.

40 Erik Sherman, "College Tuition Is Rising at Twice the Inflation Rate —While Students Learn At Home," *Forbes* (August 31, 2020), online at: https://www.forbes.com/sites/zengernews/2020/08/31/college-tuition-is-rising-at-twice-the-inflation-rate-while-students-learn-at-home/?sh=239af1302f98.

41 Helen Lewis, "What Happens When Politicians Brush Off Hard Questions About Gender," *The Atlantic* (February 15, 2023), online: <https://www.theatlantic.com/ideas/archive/2023/02/nicola-sturgeon-resignation-scotland-transgender-bill/673067/>.

42 Lal Zimman, "Trans self-identification and the language of neoliberal selfhood: Agency, power, and the limits of monologic discourse," *International Journal of the Sociology of Language* (February 25, 2019).

43 See, e.g., Employment Equity Act, SC 1995, c 44.

44 See, e.g., Geoff Leo, Carrie Bourrassa, who claimed to be Indigenous without evidence, has resigned from U of Sask, CBC (June 1, 2022), online: <https://www.cbc.ca/news/canada/saskatchewan/carrie-bourassa-resigns-1.6473964>; Liam Brittan, UBC regrets its handling of Turpel-Lafond ancestry concerns, CBC (Jan. 17, 2023), online: <https://www.cbc.ca/news/canada/british-columbia/mary-ellen-turpel-lafond-ubc-1.6717467>; and Ella Nilson, New evidence has emerged Elizabeth Warren claimed American Indian heritage in 1986, Vox (Feb. 5, 2019), online: <https://www.vox.com/2018/10/16/17983250/elizabeth-warren-bar-application-american-indian-dna>.

45 Chris McGreal, Rachel Dolezal: "I wasn't identifying as black to upset people.

I was being me," *The Guardian* (Dec. 13, 2015), online: <https://www.theguardian.com/us-news/2015/dec/13/rachel-dolezal-i-wasnt-identifying-as-black-to-upset-people-i-was-being-me>.

46 Nicholas Serafin, In Defense of Immutability, *BYU Law Review* (2020) 2.
47 Yascha Mounk, The Great Experiment: Why Democracies Fall Apart and How They Can Endure (2022), Penguin Random House LLC: New York at 83.
48 Kenji Yoshino, Covering: The Hidden Assault on Our Civil Rights, Random House Trade Paperbacks (2007).

Chapter Four

1 Abby Green, "How much is Grimsby council spending on Integrity Commissioner reports?" NiagaraThisWeek.com (March 25, 2023), online at: https://www.niagarathisweek.com/news/council/how-much-is-grimsby-council-spending-on-integrity-commissioner-reports/article_fd0fd9f1-97f8-5e19-8284-9c9ae36315ba.html.
2 Don Mitchell, "Niagara Falls to charge $200 fee for integrity complaints," Global News (Sept. 17, 2020), online at: https://globalnews.ca/news/7341381/niagara-falls-integrity-complaint/.
3 Ron Ellis, Unjust by Design: Canada's Administrative Justice System, UBC Press (2013) at 37
4 Ron Ellis, Unjust by Design: Canada's Administrative Justice System, UBC Press (2013) at 39.
5 Pelletier v. Canada (Attorney General), 2008 FCA 1.
6 "Rule 1.3 Diligence–Comment," American Bar Association, online: https://www.americanbar.org/groups/professional_responsibility/publications/model_rules_of_professional_conduct/rule_1_3_diligence/comment_on_rule_1_3/.
7 Andrew H. Friedman and Courtney Abrams, "Attorney Workplace Investigations: Neither Impartial Nor Independent," California Labor and Employer Law Review (Sept. 2022).
8 Andrew H. Friedman and Courtney Abrams, "Attorney Workplace Investigations: Neither Impartial Nor Independent," California Labor and Employer Law Review (Sept. 2022).
9 Sam Wang, "The Great Gerrymander of 2012," NYT (Feb. 2, 2013), online: https://www.nytimes.com/2013/02/03/opinion/sunday/the-great-gerrymander-of-2012.html.
10 "Boundaries for Texas's 2nd United States Federal Congressional District," Wikipedia (2013), online: https://en.wikipedia.org/wiki/Texas%27s_2nd_congressional_district#/media/File:Texas_US_Congressional_District_2_(since_2013).tif.
11 Adam Cotter, "Public confidence in Canadian institutions," Statistics Canada (December 7, 2015), online at: https://www150.statcan.gc.ca/n1/pub/89-652-x/89-652-x2015007-eng.htm

Chapter Five

1 Avanthika Anand, "OPP officer found guilty of sexually assaulting unconscious woman and filming it," CBC (April 1, 2023), online: https://www.cbc.ca/news/canada/ottawa/opp-officer-sexual-assault-jason-redmond-1.6797839.

2 R v. Redmond, 2018 ONSC 4487, [2018] OJ No. 3936.
3 Sabrina Bedford, "Sentencing delayed for OPP officer convicted of sexual assault," Ottawa Citizen (April 14, 2023), online: https://ottawacitizen.com/news/local-news/sentencing-delayed-for-opp-officer-convicted-of-sexual-assault.
4 Mark Feffer, "The Best Way to Avoid Frivolous Legal Actions Is to Communicate," SHRM (May 30, 2017), online at: https://www.shrm.org/resourcesandtools/legal-and-compliance/employment-law/pages/avoiding-frivolous-actions.aspx.
5 Ahmad, Sara, Complaint!, Duke University Press (2021) at 81.
6 Tim Petruk, "Milovick identified as TRU administrator cleared in workplace harassment investigation," Castanet (Jan. 19, 2023), online: https://www.castanetkamloops.net/news/Kamloops/407180/Milovick-identified-as-TRU-administrator-cleared-in-workplace-harassment-investigation.
7 "Q&As on Campus Sexual Misconduct," US Dept. of Education (September 2017), online: https://www2.ed.gov/about/offices/list/ocr/docs/qa-title-ix-201709.pdf.
8 Eiffel's Tower: The Thrilling Story Behind Paris's Beloved Monument and the Extraordinary World's Fair That Introduced It.
9 Brian Potter, "How NEPA works," Construction Physics (Aug. 19, 2022), online: https://www.construction-physics.com/p/how-nepa-works.
10 Brian Potter, "How NEPA works," Construction Physics (Aug. 19, 2022), online: https://www.construction-physics.com/p/how-nepa-works.
11 Mary Douglas and Aaron Wildavsky, Risk and Culture: An Essay on the Selection of Technological and Environmental Dangers, University of California Press (1983) at 3.
12 Aaron Wildavsky, Searching for Safety, Routledge (2017) at 57.
13 Aaron Wildavsky, Searching for Safety, Routledge (2017) at 57.
14 Aaron Wildavsky, Searching for Safety, Routledge (2017) at 73.
15 Phillip K. Howard, Death of Common Sense: How Law Is Suffocating America, Grand Central Publish (1996).
16 Ipsos, Sexual Harassment Survey (Oct. 2018), online: https://www.ipsos.com/sites/default/files/ct/news/documents/2018-10/npr-sexual_harassment-tables.pdf.
17 "AN ACT to amend Tennessee Code Annotated, Title 49, Chapter 7, relative to higher education," Tennessee House of Representatives (April 13, 2022), online: https://legiscan.com/TN/amendment/HB2670/id/131285.
18 "AN ACT to amend Tennessee Code Annotated, Title 49, Chapter 7, relative to higher education," Tennessee House of Representatives (April 13, 2022), online: https://legiscan.com/TN/amendment/HB2670/id/131285.
19 "AN ACT to amend Tennessee Code Annotated, Title 49, Chapter 7, relative to higher education," Tennessee House of Representatives (April 13, 2022), online: https://legiscan.com/TN/amendment/HB2670/id/131285.

Chapter Six

1 Rex v. Sussex Justices, [1924] 1 KB 256, Lord Hewart CJ.
2 Seventh Annual Employee Relations Benchmark Study," HRAcuity (May 2023) at 9.
3 Tim Petruk, "Milovick identified as TRU administrator cleared in workplace harassment investigation," Castanet (Jan. 19, 2023), online: https://www.castanetkamloops.net/news/Kamloops/407180/Milovick-identified-as-TRU-administrator-cleared-in-workplace-harassment-investigation.
4 Paul James, "TRU finds 'wrongdoing,' but takes no action, following misconduct

probe into senior University leaders," Radio NL 610 AM (Jan. 17, 2023), online at: https://www.radionl.com/2023/01/17/tru-investigation-finds-wrongdoing-as-part-of/ and Thompson Rivers University, "Budget Model" (accessed online July 1, 2023), online at: https://www.tru.ca/vpadmin/budget.html.

5   Thompson Rivers University, "Board of Governors Investigation" (accessed online July 1, 2023), online at: https://www.tru.ca/board/board-of-governors-investigation.html.

6   Tim Petruk, "Defamation lawsuit filed by TRU VP against accusers in high-profile misconduct probe," Castanet (Feb. 10, 2023), online: https://www.castanetkamloops.net/news/Kamloops/410773/Defamation-lawsuit-filed-by-TRU-VP-against-accusers-in-high-profile-misconduct-probe.

7   Tim Petruk, "Defamation lawsuit filed by TRU VP against accusers in high-profile misconduct probe," Castanet (Feb. 10, 2023), online: https://www.castanetkamloops.net/news/Kamloops/410773/Defamation-lawsuit-filed-by-TRU-VP-against-accusers-in-high-profile-misconduct-probe.

8   A-2015-00007, CBC, online at: https://site-cbc.radio-canada.ca/documents/impact-and-accountability/ati/contracts/a-2015-00007.pdf.

9   "ERMA Investigators," Employment Risk Management Authority (May 2023), online at: https://www.ermajpa.org/wp-content/uploads/2022/01/ERMA-List-of-Investigators-January-2022.pdf.

10 Association of Workplace Investigators, "Guiding Principles for Conducting Workplace Investigations."

11 Application for Leave to Obtain Direct Appellate Review, pg. 14, April 15, 2020, DAR-27419.

12 Facebook, Inc., "Form S-1 Registration Statement," United States Securities Exchange Commission, Feb. 1, 2012.

13 Id.

14 Application for Leave to Obtain Direct Appellate Review, pg. 14, April 15, 2020, DAR-27419.

15 Mem. of Law in Supp. of the AG's Pet. to Compel Comp. with Civ. Inv. Demand, pg. 1, Oct. 15, 2019, 1984CV02597-BLS.

16 Id.

17 Mem. of Law in Supp. of the AG's Pet. to Compel Comp. with Civ. Inv. Demand, pgs. 5-6, Oct. 15, 2019, 1984CV02597-BLS.

18 Id. at pg. 6.

19 Application for Leave to Obtain Direct Appellate Review, pg. 15, April 15, 2020, DAR-27419.

20 Decision and Order Regarding Attorney General's Petition to Compel Compliance with Civil Investigative Demand Pursuant to G.L. c. 93A, § 7, pg. 4, Jan. 17, 2020, 1984CV02597-BLS1.

21 Matthew Rosenberg, Nicholas Confessore, and Carole Cadwalladr, "How Trump Consultants Exploited the Facebook Data of Millions," The New York Times, March 17, 2018.

22 Paul Lewis and Paul Hilder, "Leaked: Cambridge Analytica's blueprint for Trump victory," The Guardian, March 23, 2018.

23 Id.

24 Carole Cadwalladr and Emma Graham-Harrison, "Revealed: 50 million Facebook profiles harvested for Cambridge Analytica in major data breach," The Guardian, March 17, 2018 and Matthew Rosenberg, Nicholas Confessore, and Carole Cadwalladr, "How Trump Consultants Exploited the Facebook Data of Millions," The New York Times, March 17, 2018; Kozlowska, Hanna, "The Cambridge Analytica

scandal affected nearly 40 million more people than we thought," *Quartz*, April 4, 2018.

25 Ime Archibong, "Facebook Platform Changes in Development," Facebook for Developers, March 26, 2018. The changes in 2014 refer to the introduction of changes to the Login feature, which permitted users to elect logging into apps without sharing their information—something they previously could not do.

26 Rodriguez, Salvador, "Here are the scandals and other incidents that have sent Facebook's share price tanking in 2018," CNBC, November 20, 2018.

27 Tiffany Hsu, "For Many Facebook Users, a 'Last Straw' That Led Them to Quit," *NYT* (March 21, 2018), online: https://www.nytimes.com/2018/03/21/technology/users-abandon-facebook.html.

28 Chloe Watson, "The key moments from Mark Zuckerberg's testimony to Congress," *The Guardian*, April 11, 2018.

29 Id.

30 Facebook, "An Update on Our App Investigation and Audit," May 14, 2018. (Reiterating Zuckerberg's comments "[t]he investigation process is in full swing, and it has two phases. First, a comprehensive review to identify every app that had access to this amount of Facebook data. And second, where we have concerns, we will conduct interviews, make requests for information (RFI)—which ask a series of detailed questions about the app and the data it has access to—and perform audits that may include on-site inspections.")

31 Salvador Rodriguez, "Facebook has suspended tens of thousands of apps after the Cambridge Analytica investigation," CNBC, Sept. 20, 2019.

32 Attorney General v. Facebook, Inc., Mass. Sup. J. C. (SJC-12946) (March 24, 2021) at 2.

33 Application for Leave to Obtain Direct Appellate Review, pg. 17, April 15, 2020, DAR-27419.

34 Attorney General v. Facebook, Inc., Mass. S. J. C. March 24, 2021, at 9 (SJC-12946).

35 Id.

36 Eric Moskowitz, "AG Healey announces investigation into data firm used by Trump campaign," *Boston Globe*, March 17, 2018. For the announcement on Twitter, see also https://twitter.com/massago/status/975052674818347013. See also: https://twitter.com/massago/status/975052674818347013. The law was G.L. c. 93A, sec. 8.

37 Mem. of Law in Supp. of the AG's Pet. to Compel Comp. with Civ. Inv. Demand, pg. 1, Oct. 15, 2019, 1984CV02597-BLS.

38 Brief for Petitioner-Appellee AG Maura Healey, pg. 22, Sept. 30, 2020, No. SJC-12946.

39 Brief for Petitioner-Appellee AG Maura Healey, pg. 22–23, Sept. 30, 2020, No. SJC-12946.

40 Application for Leave to Obtain Direct Appellate Review, pg. 18, April 15, 2020, DAR-27419. (Original emphasis).

41 Application for Leave to Obtain Direct Appellate Review, pg. 11, April 15, 2020, DAR-27419.

42 Id. (Internal citations omitted).

43 Attorney General v. Facebook, Inc., Mass. Sup. J. C. (SJC-12946) (March 24, 2021) at 35.

44 Attorney General v. Facebook, Inc., Mass. Sup. J. C. (SJC-12946) (March 24, 2021) at 35.

45 Attorney General v. Facebook, Inc., Mass. Sup. J. C. (SJC-12946) (March 24, 2021) at 35.

46 Attorney General v. Facebook, Inc., Mass. Sup. J. C. (SJC-12946) (March 24, 2021) at 35 at fn. 20.

Chapter Seven

1 Don Mitchell, "Niagara Falls to charge $200 fee for integrity complaints," Global News (Sept. 17, 2020), online at: https://globalnews.ca/news/7341381/niagara-falls-integrity-complaint/.

2 Anna Brown, "More Than Twice as Many Americans Support Than Oppose the #MeToo Movement," Pew Research Center (Sept. 29, 2022), online at: https://www.pewresearch.org/social-trends/2022/09/29/more-than-twice-as-many-americans-support-than-oppose-the-metoo-movement/.

3 Mark Gollom, "Jian Ghomeshi found not guilty on choking and all sex assault charges," CBC (March 24, 2016), online at: https://www.cbc.ca/news/canada/toronto/jian-ghomeshi-sexual-assault-trial-ruling-1.3505446.

4 Robin Doolitte, Had It Coming: What's Fair in the Age of #MeToo? (2019), Allen Lane.